Bitcoin

MASTERING THE WORLD OF CRYPTOCURRENCY:

YOUR ULTIMATE HANDBOOK ON BITCOIN

Felix Ryder

TABLE OF CONTENTS

INTRODUCTION

Welcome to "Bitcoin: Mastering the World of Cryptocurrency - Your Ultimate Handbook on Bitcoin". This e-book is your in-depth guide to the intriguing world of Bitcoin and the larger cryptocurrency landscape. This guide is created to meet your needs, whether you're a curious beginner trying to grasp what all the fuss is about, a casual trader looking to expand your knowledge, or an experienced investor looking to stay on the cutting edge of the crypto world.

The financial industry is evolving from what we once knew. There are now other ways to carry out transactions, make investments, and store value besides using traditional fiat currencies. A new type of decentralized digital currency built on the blockchain technology was made possible by the 2009 invention of Bitcoin. In addition to being well-known today, Bitcoin also sparked a technological revolution and gave rise to dozens of alternative cryptocurrencies.

Even for tech-savvy people, navigating this novel area of decentralized finance can be challenging. The technology can seem impenetrable, the terms are frequently cryptic, and the environment is always shifting. This e-book fills that need.

In this e-book, we begin with the very basics of Bitcoin: the issue it sought to address, the idea behind it, and the technology it is based on. We will discuss the mechanisms underlying Bitcoin transactions, mining, and value maintenance. The significance of wallets, keys, and addresses on the Bitcoin network will be explained to you, and we'll walk you through the purchasing, selling, and using procedures.

We will also go in-depth on Bitcoin trading and investment strategies, giving you an understanding of various methods and risk-management techniques. The e-book will provide you an overview of the wider world of cryptocurrencies, explain how Bitcoin interacts with "altcoins," and go over some key forks in Bitcoin's past.

Finally, this guide will discuss crucial issues related to privacy, security, and the legal implications of using Bitcoin before offering expert predictions about this revolutionary currency's future.

So be ready for an educational adventure through the exciting and dynamic world of Bitcoin. Here is where the path to mastering Bitcoin begins!

CHAPTER
I
Bitcoin:
The Genesis of Cryptocurrency

What is Bitcoin?

Bitcoin, a decentralized digital currency, has become extremely popular since emerging from the financial crisis of 2008. As the first cryptocurrency, Bitcoin challenges established financial systems by providing a peer-to-peer network free of intermediaries and authorities. Bitcoin is based on cryptographic proof, enabling transactions that are safe, verifiable, and irreversible. It was conceptualized by the pseudonym entity, Satoshi Nakamoto. The intricate nature of Bitcoin will be examined in this section, along with its underlying technology, guiding principles, and ability to completely alter the way we think about money.

In a white paper titled "Bitcoin: A Peer-to-Peer Electronic Cash System," which Nakamoto released in October 2008, the idea for Bitcoin was described. The Genesis Block or Block 0 of the Bitcoin blockchain, which is the first block, was not mined by Nakamoto until January 3, 2009. Bitcoin emerged as a symbol of hope for a decentralized financial future in the wake of a failing financial system marred by bank bailouts and mistrust.

With Bitcoin, the use of a reliable third party like banks or governments in financial transactions was intended to be eliminated. Bitcoin suggests a radical reinvention of financial systems by establishing a system where trust is generated not by strong intermediaries but rather by network consensus, cryptography, and innovative software.

At its foundation, Bitcoin is a cryptocurrency that uses cryptographic methods to protect transactions, limit the creation of new units, and confirm the transfer of assets. Bitcoin is decentralized and relies on a dispersed network of users to carry out and validate transactions, in contrast to conventional currencies (fiat currencies) that are issued by a centralized authority.

The blockchain technology, on which Bitcoin is based, is one of its mainstays. A public, decentralized ledger called the blockchain stores all Bitcoin transactions. Each transaction is collected into a single "block," which is then included in the "chain" of previous transactions. As changing any transaction record in the chain would require an unlikely majority consensus from the entire network, this process ensures transparency and security.

The act of "mining" is a crucial component of Bitcoin's operations. In essence, this involves using processing power to solve difficult mathematical puzzles before adding the results to the blockchain to validate the transactions. The phrase "mining" refers to the process of creating new bitcoins as a reward, along with transaction fees.

The rate at which new Bitcoin are created is likewise managed by this process. Every four years, or "the halvening," the network is structured to reduce the mining return by half. Due to this system's falling rate of production, there will only ever be about 21 million bitcoins in circulation, giving bitcoin a scarcity that is comparable to that of precious commodities like gold.

The organization of bitcoin transactions is distinct. Bitcoin transactions take place between 'addresses' as opposed to traditional transactions, where identities are connected to accounts. Similar to an account number, a Bitcoin address is a collection of alphanumeric characters that designates the recipient of a Bitcoin payment.

A corresponding private key must be held in order to control the bitcoins linked to an address. Similar to a digital signature, this private key ensures a transaction's legitimacy and prevents it from being changed once it has been authorized.

These addresses and private keys are managed by users using 'wallets' for bitcoin. They can take a lot of different forms, from hardware to mobile apps, and offer various degrees of convenience and security.

Bitcoin is fundamentally different from conventional types of currency due to its features and design. It offers a level of user autonomy and privacy uncommon in conventional banking systems due to its decentralized nature. Its inherent scarcity mechanism challenges the fiat currencies' tendency to inflate, giving it a potential "store of value" similar to gold.

However, due to Bitcoin's relative infancy and its volatile price, its usefulness as a "medium of exchange" has come under investigation. Bitcoin is becoming more and more accepted by merchants, although its widespread use as a payment method is still in its early stages.

Understanding Bitcoin necessitates an appreciation for its technological complexity, decentralized ethos, and potential to fundamentally alter how we view and use money. Bitcoin's journey has been characterized by volatility, scrutiny, and, more recently, gaining acceptance from its conception to its current significance. It now serves as a representation of a larger movement towards decentralization and financial digital change, serving as an inspiration for countless other blockchain and cryptocurrency projects.

In essence, Bitcoin is a socio-economic experiment in trust, decentralization, and digital scarcity rather than merely a digital asset or currency. Bitcoin serves as a reminder and a tool of financial self-sovereignty and transparency as we head towards a more digital future. It symbolizes a change in how we see, utilize, and interact with money.

History of Bitcoin and the problem it aimed to solve

The world experienced a severe financial crisis in the latter part of the 2000s. A severe economic downturn caused by unprecedented bank failures, risky lending practices, and complex financial products shook trust in conventional financial institutions. In response to these issues, Bitcoin surfaced, trying to address the fundamental issues with conventional financial systems. This section digs into the origins of Bitcoin and considers the particular issues it was intended to solve.

The origins of Bitcoin are a mystery. A white paper titled "Bitcoin: A Peer-to-Peer Electronic Cash System" was released in 2008 under the pseudonym Satoshi Nakamoto by an unidentified person or group. The theoretical foundation for a decentralized digital currency, which would later become Bitcoin, was spelled forth in this white paper. The "genesis block" or "block 0"—also known as the first block of the Bitcoin blockchain—was mined by Nakamoto on January 3, 2009. This was the beginning of Bitcoin.

This event was noteworthy not just because a new kind of money was created, but also because it represented a form of opposition to the failing financial system. The text "The Times 03/Jan/2009

Chancellor on brink of second bailout for banks" from a headline in The Times newspaper was encoded into the genesis block. This was a clear indication that Bitcoin was a reaction to both the uncertain economic environment and the perceived shortcomings of conventional financial institutions.

The foundation of the conventional financial system is trust. We trust banks to store and manage our money, payment processors to move it, and governments to protect its purchasing power. But the financial crisis of 2008 showed how this trust might be misplaced.

This trust issue is what led to the creation of Bitcoin. The blockchain technology is at the center of the Bitcoin design. A public ledger that keeps track of all Bitcoin transactions is called the blockchain. Using a decentralized network of computers (called nodes), this system functions without the aid of a central authority.

Nodes verify transactions through a consensus mechanism, doing so without the need of a reliable third party. This idea, known as "trustless" transactions, is ground-breaking since it eliminates the need for intermediaries and makes peer-to-peer transactions possible on a worldwide scale.

Financial systems are centralized by nature. Governments oversee the financial environment, central banks control monetary policy, and commercial banks handle transactions. This concentration makes it possible to manage people's finances. Bitcoin uses decentralization to try to solve this issue.

Bitcoin makes sure that no single body can control the Bitcoin protocol because it is a decentralized network. It resists censorship and gives even those who are excluded by conventional banking systems a way to participate in the economy.

The rising supply of traditional currencies can lead to inflation. The ability of central banks to produce additional money might result in currency devaluation. The fixed supply of Bitcoin coins, on the other hand, is around 21 million. Since this limit is hard-coded into the Bitcoin system, it creates scarcity and may eventually turn Bitcoin into a reliable store of value. With this approach, we want to solve the issue of currency devaluation that the conventional monetary system has.

The response to issues in conventional banking systems has played a significant role in Bitcoin's history. Out of the ashes of the financial crisis of 2008, Bitcoin arose as a ground-breaking remedy intended to address problems with trust, centralization, and inflation in financial institutions. Its capacity to offer a decentralized, peer-to-peer payment system, where confidence is built through cryptographic proof rather than through central authorities, is what gives it its revolutionary potential.

Despite the appreciation and criticism it has received over the years, Bitcoin's roots are still closely related to its initial objective: to offer an alternative to the traditional financial system and transform how we view and use money. As we proceed, it's critical to keep in mind the issues that Bitcoin sought to resolve, as they provide a key to comprehending the value proposition of this revolutionary technology.

The pseudonymous creator: Satoshi Nakamoto

Nobody is more mysterious and consequential in the world of cryptocurrencies than Satoshi Nakamoto. This unidentified person or group is credited for creating Bitcoin, the first decentralized cryptocurrency in the world, which profoundly changed the face of money and technology. Despite Bitcoin's extensive influence and acceptance, its creator's identity is still a mystery, giving rise to much speculation and curiosity. The history of Satoshi Nakamoto, their important achievements, and the ongoing mysteries regarding their identity are all covered in this section.

The publication of a white paper titled "Bitcoin: A Peer-to-Peer Electronic Cash System" in 2008 marks the beginning of Satoshi Nakamoto's tale. The theoretical foundation for Bitcoin, a revolutionary kind of digital money, was put out in this nine-page document. Nakamoto created Bitcoin by mining the initial block of the blockchain on January 3, 2009, a few months later.

For approximately two years, Nakamoto continued to contribute actively to the development of Bitcoin, corresponding with other programmers and collaborators through emails and forum posts. In this period, Nakamoto's writings showed a person who was strongly committed to the concept of a decentralized currency system free from censorship and government oversight.

Beyond merely conceptualizing Bitcoin, Nakamoto made significant contributions. They contributed to the development of the Bitcoin software's source code and kept improving and updating it until their final recorded communication in 2010. Nakamoto is credited with the invention of the proof-of-work algorithm and the decentralized consensus system, among other ground-breaking ideas and innovations.

The blockchain, which is the most innovative aspect of Bitcoin, was created by Nakamoto. All Bitcoin transactions are recorded in this decentralized public ledger, which enables trustless peer-to-peer transactions and represents a major breakthrough in digital trust and security.

The originator of the pseudonym "Satoshi Nakamoto" cannot be found, and there are no hints as to his or her identity, nationality, or location. Due to this anonymity and the influence of Bitcoin, there has been a lot of speculation and research done to identify the person or organization hiding behind the alias. Several individuals have been put forward as the real Satoshi, and some have even claimed to be him or her. Nakamoto's identity is still a mystery because none of these assertions or charges have been proved beyond a reasonable doubt.

The last known communication from Nakamoto came in December 2010, in which they said they had "moved on to other things" and that Bitcoin was "in good hands" going forward. After that, Nakamoto vanished entirely from the public view, handing over control of Bitcoin to the growing community of developers and enthusiasts.

Nakamoto's impact on Bitcoin and the broader cryptocurrency industry continues despite their disappearance. Their goal of creating a decentralized, peer-to-peer electronic cash system has not only been realized, but it has also generated a wave of creativity that has produced thousands of alternative cryptocurrencies and innovative blockchain-based applications.

The developer of Bitcoin under the alias Satoshi Nakamoto is a mysterious and intriguing individual. Despite their secrecy, their ground-breaking idea has produced a lasting impact on technology and money. A new era of technological innovation and disruption has been brought in by Nakamoto's idea of a decentralized financial system. Even though their identity is still a mystery, their influence is undeniable and hasn't stopped resonating throughout the online community. Nakamoto's Bitcoin has revolutionized the way we think about and engage with finance by posing difficult questions about the nature of money, trust, and decentralization.

The Bitcoin whitepaper: A brief summary

A nine-page document titled "Bitcoin: A Peer-to-Peer Electronic Cash System," written by the mysterious author Satoshi Nakamoto, is where the invention of Bitcoin, a revolutionary digital asset, may be found. This ground-breaking report, released in 2008, presents the conceptual underpinning for Bitcoin and suggests a significant redesign of traditional financial institutions. This section provides a thorough analysis of the Bitcoin whitepaper, emphasizing its important recommendations and advancements in the fields of cryptocurrencies and blockchain technology.

The dependence on financial institutions to process electronic payments is the fundamental issue with internet commerce, which is addressed in the opening section of Nakamoto's whitepaper. To avoid duplicate spending, which occurs when a user spends the same amount twice, traditional electronic currency systems need the assistance of a reliable third party. Without a trustworthy third party, Nakamoto suggested Bitcoin as a solution to the double-spending issue.

A peer-to-peer kind of electronic cash, according to Nakamoto, bitcoin enables internet payments to be transmitted directly from one party to another without passing through a financial institution.

Nakamoto saw trust as the primary problem with conventional financial transactions. Because copies of digital tokens can be created and used in many transactions, there is a risk of double spending in digital transactions.

In response, Nakamoto offered a peer-to-peer network approach to the double-spending issue. Transactions are timestamped by the network and hashed into a continuous chain of hash-based proof-of-work to create a record that cannot be altered without repeating the proof-of-work. The blockchain technology that supports Bitcoin is built on top of this.

The Bitcoin whitepaper spends a lot of time describing the mining process. Verifying and adding transaction records to the blockchain, the open ledger for Bitcoin, is known as mining. Multiple nodes compete to solve challenging mathematical puzzles in a decentralized approach.

Bitcoins are given to miners as payment for their work validating transactions. The incentive has two functions: it encourages nodes to maintain their integrity and it adds additional bitcoins to the system, creating a sort of "gold rush."

The principles of security and privacy in the Bitcoin network are also covered by Nakamoto. The identity of the people involved in the transactions are kept secret, despite the fact that the transaction flow is public and transparent on the blockchain. This is accomplished by utilizing cryptographic methods that guarantee anonymity.

Despite being only a few pages long, the Bitcoin whitepaper proposes a ground-breaking idea that goes against the very foundations of conventional financial institutions. In addition to giving birth to Bitcoin, Nakamoto's design for a decentralized, peer-to-peer electronic cash system also gave birth to blockchain, a brand-new area of technology.

Decentralization, cryptographic proof, and digital scarcity are key ideas that were first articulated in the whitepaper and are now guiding ideas for many blockchain and cryptocurrency initiatives. The underlying philosophy of Bitcoin, as outlined in the whitepaper, continues to motivate and inspire innovation in the field of digital finance even though the journey toward its creation has not been without its challenges.

CHAPTER
II
Understanding the Basics of Cryptocurrency

What is a cryptocurrency?

Throughout its history, the world of finance has experienced a number of significant transformational events, but maybe none as ground-breaking as the introduction of cryptocurrencies. After the invention of Bitcoin, the first digital currency to function decentralized, the word "cryptocurrency" gained widespread recognition. There are thousands of digital currencies available on the market today, each with its own features and uses. This section examines the idea of cryptocurrencies, the technology that underpins them, and its implications for financial systems and other areas.

A digital or virtual currency known as a cryptocurrency uses cryptography to ensure its security. It uses blockchain technology, which is a decentralized platform for recording all transactions over a network of computers. Because cryptocurrencies are not issued by a single entity, they are theoretically shielded from interference or manipulation by governments.

The current state of cryptocurrencies is the result of the integration of various academic fields, including computer science, encryption, and economics. These factors were brought together in the development of Bitcoin, the first widely used cryptocurrency, to produce a special remedy for the issue of digital trust.

Blockchain is a technology that underpins Bitcoin and the majority of other cryptocurrencies. It essentially functions as a distributed ledger of all transactions that is accessible to anybody on the network. The network is not under the control of a single body due to its decentralization, which is crucial.

Typically, cryptocurrencies are produced through a process called mining, in which powerful computers carry out intricate computations to verify network transactions. Miners are paid for their labor with fresh coins, which motivates them to keep working. This procedure adds fresh currencies to the bitcoin ecosystem while also assisting in network security.

Cryptocurrencies are fundamentally intended to serve as a form of exchange, just like conventional currencies. They can be used to make online purchases of goods and services, with more companies accepting bitcoin payments.

Additionally, some cryptocurrencies, such as Bitcoin, are frequently seen as a store of value, much like gold. This impression is a result of their inherent scarcity; the system has a hard limit of 21 million bitcoins.

Significant implications have been brought about by the emergence of cryptocurrencies. On the other hand, they present enticing possibilities, such as the possibility of financial inclusion for unbanked populations, reduced transaction fees than typical online payment systems, and the development of decentralized applications, to mention a few.

Cryptocurrencies do, however, also come with some difficulties. Their anonymity might make illegal actions like tax evasion or money laundering easier. Additionally, the value of cryptocurrencies has the ability to fluctuate greatly, putting investors at risk of losing money.

In the field of finance, cryptocurrencies represent a paradigm change. They take on established financial systems and provide an alternative form of currency by creating a decentralized, peer-to-peer electronic cash system. They have a great potential to change the way we think about money, make financial inclusion possible, and promote technological advancement.

However, how effectively they can navigate the legal environment, technological barriers, and public acceptance will determine their adoption and ultimate success. The evolution and implications of cryptocurrencies demand particular attention as the digital era progresses. They represent the power of invention and might be a sign of a future with decentralized finance; they are more than just digital money.

The blockchain technology: An introduction

The idea that supports the operation of cryptocurrencies like Bitcoin is known as blockchain technology, which is often regarded as one of the most significant technological innovations of the 21st century. However, it has much more potential than just digital currencies, and it has the ability to revolutionize many different industries. This section aims to provide an introduction to blockchain technology by examining its inner workings, prospective uses, and implications for the digital future.

A blockchain is fundamentally a distributed ledger of transactions that is duplicated and kept on a network of computers known as nodes. Every time a new transaction takes place on the blockchain, a record of that transaction is recorded to every participant's ledger. Each block comprises a number of transactions.

No one entity has power over the entire chain due to the network's decentralized structure. The word "blockchain" refers to the chain of blocks that is formed by each block in the chain, which also includes a cryptographic hash of the one before it. The ledger is tamper-resistant and offers a reliable record of transactions due to this cryptographic linking.

The decentralized nature of blockchain technology is one of its primary features. A blockchain network is distributed among several nodes, unlike traditional databases, which are normally managed by a single institution. This makes sure that no single node can alter the data saved on the blockchain.

Transparency is another key feature of blockchain over conventional methods. Every transaction on the network is accessible to all users, resulting in a transparent system where any node can confirm a transaction's legitimacy.

Advanced cryptography is used by blockchain technology to guarantee data security and integrity. Each block includes transaction information, a timestamp, and a cryptographic hash of the one before it. Because of the blocks' cryptographic connections, it is impossible to alter the transaction data contained within a block without also altering all future blocks.

The potential of blockchain technology goes beyond simply preserving transactional information. 'Smart contracts' and decentralized apps (DApps) are now conceivable because of the development of programmable blockchains.

Smart contracts are agreements that automatically carry out their obligations because they are encoded in code. They cut out the intermediaries by automatically completing transactions when certain conditions are met.

Decentralized applications, or DApps, are independent of any single authority and operate on a blockchain network in a public, open-source, decentralized environment.

Digital transactions are now more decentralized, transparent, and secure because of the development of blockchain technology. Blockchain represents a significant improvement in the way we handle and record transactions with its potential applications across industries including finance, supply chain management, healthcare, and more.

Blockchain technology is still in its infancy, however, and faces difficulties like scalability problems, regulatory uncertainties, and adoption restrictions. This is despite the fact that it has enormous potential. The final influence of blockchain on society and the digital world is still unknown, but there is no denying that it has enormous potential for transformation.

Understanding cryptography in cryptocurrency

Numerous technological developments, of which cryptography has a major role, have made it possible for cryptocurrencies to emerge as a new class of digital assets. The foundation of cryptocurrency is cryptography, which ensures safe transactions and controls the generation of new units. Cryptography is the practice and study of secure communication in the presence of adversaries. This section explores the complex world of cryptography in cryptocurrencies, as well as its use and effects.

Cryptography has two important functions in the context of cryptocurrencies like Bitcoin: it controls the generation of new coins and ensures that transactions between parties are secure. In short, encryption in cryptocurrencies enables users to store money securely and make payments without using their name or going through a bank.

A mechanism known as public key cryptography is one of the main ways encryption is employed in cryptocurrencies. Each user in this system has two keys: a public key that is made public and serves as an address for receiving cryptocurrency, and a private key that is kept private and is used to approve transactions.

The sender signs a transaction using both their private key and the recipient's public key when a transaction is started. Using the sender's public key, the network authenticates the transaction to make sure it came from them. This procedure guarantees the transactions' legitimacy and integrity, protecting them against fraud.

The use of cryptographic hash functions in cryptocurrencies, particularly in the development of the blockchain, is another crucial use of cryptography. A hash function accepts an input and outputs a fixed-size string of bytes, usually a hash code. Each unique input yields a different hash as the output.

A chain of blocks is formed in blockchain because each block has a hash of the one before it. Since changing any information in a block will change its hash and influence all succeeding blocks in the chain, this renders the blockchain tamper-evident.

Cryptographic concepts play a significant role in the mining process for cryptocurrencies, especially proof-of-work systems like Bitcoin. Complex cryptographic puzzles must be solved by miners, which takes a lot of processing power. The first miner to complete the problem is given the opportunity to add a new block to the blockchain and receive a reward in cryptocurrency.

The foundation upon which the idea of cryptocurrency depends is cryptography. It secures user identities, offers security, integrity, and authentication for transactions, and controls the issuance of new currency.

Despite how reliable cryptographic methods are, it is important to remember that they do not completely eliminate the risks involved in bitcoin transactions. Cryptocurrency security is just as strong as the security measures taken by their users. Private keys must be protected with care, and participants in transactions must use caution.

The importance of cryptography in maintaining security and trust in the virtual world is anticipated to grow as the digital age goes on. Cryptocurrencies serve as a compelling example of how these complex mathematical approaches can be applied to build a system where confidence is established through mathematics and code rather than intermediaries.

CHAPTER
III
Digging Deeper:
The Bitcoin Network

How does Bitcoin work?

A decentralized, peer-to-peer digital currency was first successfully implemented with Bitcoin, which has come to represent all cryptocurrencies. Since its creation in 2008 by a person or group of people using the pseudonym Satoshi Nakamoto, it has completely changed how the world views money and financial activities. The operation of Bitcoin will be examined in detail in this section, including with its underlying technology, transactional flow, and idea of mining.

Blockchain is a revolutionary piece of technology that powers Bitcoin. The blockchain is a decentralized, open ledger that keeps track of all Bitcoin transactions. A network of 'nodes', or computers, that verify and log transactions, maintains it.

Each "block" in the chain represents a collection of transaction data, and each participant's ledger is updated whenever a new transaction is made. The word "blockchain" refers to the chain of blocks that are connected by a cryptographic hash of the one before it.

Each user of Bitcoin needs two cryptographic keys in order to conduct transactions: a public key, which acts as an address that is publicly visible and to which others can transfer Bitcoin, and a private key, which is used to approve transactions and access the user's Bitcoin.

When a Bitcoin transaction is started, the sender signs a message with the input (the source transaction(s) of the coins), amount, and output (the recipient's address). They do this using their private key. The Bitcoin network then broadcasts this transaction, and miners check it before adding it to the blockchain.

The process of creating new Bitcoins and adding transactions to the blockchain is known as bitcoin mining. Powerful computers are used by miners to solve challenging mathematical puzzles that verify each transaction. The 'block reward' is the quantity of freshly created Bitcoins awarded to the first miner that solves the puzzle in exchange for adding a new block to the blockchain.

To ensure that a new block is introduced to the blockchain roughly every 10 minutes, the difficulty of these issues is adjusted every two weeks. Due to the requirement that a majority of the network's miners agree on the authenticity of transactions, this approach also ensures the decentralization of Bitcoin.

The inherent scarcity of Bitcoin is one of its most distinctive features. The number of Bitcoins that will ever be created is limited by its creator(s) to 21 million. In an event known as the "halving," the block reward, which is how new Bitcoins are added to the system, is cut in half about every four years.

One of the elements that contributes to Bitcoin's value is its inherent scarcity, which is comparable to that of precious metals like gold. Bitcoin's supply is algorithmically controlled, making it immune to inflation, in contrast to traditional fiat currencies, which can be freely printed by central banks.

A new form of currency has been envisioned due to Bitcoin's groundbreaking combination of blockchain technology, cryptographic security, and a decentralized network. Its operation, which makes use of a worldwide network of miners, ensures its security, reliability, and censorship resistance.

But there are obstacles along the way for Bitcoin, such as scalability problems, energy consumption issues, and regulatory scrutiny. A financial system where trust is generated not by centralized intermediaries but rather by networked, transparent, and auditable technology is what Bitcoin holds as it continues to develop and grow.

Explanation of terms: Bitcoin, bitcoin (capitalization difference)

Bitcoin and bitcoin are two terms that sometimes cause confusion in the field of cryptocurrency. These terms, despite having identical names, have different implications and meanings within the bitcoin ecosystem. With an emphasis on their definitions, roles, and relevance, each term will be thoroughly explained in this section. People can navigate the cryptocurrency world with clarity and precision by comprehending the differences between Bitcoin and bitcoin.

The original and most well-known cryptocurrency is called Bitcoin, with a capital "B." It was introduced in 2009 by a person or group operating under the pseudonym Satoshi Nakamoto. Bitcoin is built on the Proof-of-Work (PoW) technology and runs on the blockchain, a decentralized peer-to-peer network.

Without the use of intermediaries, peer-to-peer transactions are possible with the help of the digital currency known as Bitcoin. It has a global reach and enables users to send and receive money anonymously and securely. Transparency and immutability are provided by the blockchain used by Bitcoin.

Bitcoin operates as a decentralized digital currency that only lives online. It controls the generation of new units and secures transactions using cryptographic concepts. Because of its decentralized nature, the Bitcoin network is not governed by a single organization or authority. Through digital wallets, users may store, transmit, and receive bitcoins.

Bitcoin has significantly changed several facets of the financial landscape. It has put traditional financial structures to the test, offered an alternative to fiat money, and fostered a new era of decentralized finance. The price volatility of Bitcoin and its acceptance by institutional investors have attracted a lot of interest and funding. Numerous alternative cryptocurrencies and blockchain-based applications have been developed as a result of the innovation and potential of Bitcoin.

The smallest unit of the Bitcoin cryptocurrency is referred to as bitcoin, with a lowercase "b." Within the Bitcoin ecosystem, it serves as the unit of account and represents a portion of a Bitcoin.

The unit of account used to measure and conduct transactions with Bitcoin is bitcoin. Bitcoin is divided into satoshis, with one bitcoin equal to 100 million satoshis, much as how the dollar is divided into cents. Due to the accuracy of calculations and transactions made possible by using bitcoin as a unit of account, various quantities can be handled with flexibility.

Beyond Bitcoin itself, bitcoin serves as the unit of account. It has become extensively used as a reference point for pricing and trading other cryptocurrencies. Alternative cryptocurrencies are frequently discussed in terms of the price or value of bitcoin. In the cryptocurrency market, this practice makes comparison and evaluation simple.

Understanding the differences between Bitcoin and bitcoin is essential for comprehending their various purposes and uses. With a capital "B," the term "Bitcoin" designates the entire cryptocurrency ecosystem, including the technology, network, and digital currency itself. The lowest unit of account within that system is referred to by the lowercase word "bitcoin," on the other hand. Within the cryptocurrency community, accurate communication is ensured and misunderstandings are avoided by using the right term precisely.

An important linguistic standard that explains the meanings and contexts of the words is the capitalization difference between Bitcoin and bitcoin.

It is common to capitalize "Bitcoin" when referring to the cryptocurrency as a whole. This capitalization style highlights its position as the original cryptocurrency that popularized the idea of decentralized digital currency. It denotes the technology's broader effects and how they will affect the financial sector.

In contrast, "bitcoin" in lowercase refers solely to the unit of account used in the Bitcoin network. It is used to represent fractional amounts of the virtual money, enabling accurate valuations and transactions. When discussing various aspects of the cryptocurrency ecosystem, following the capitalization convention guarantees clarity and prevents misunderstanding.

Effective communication within the cryptocurrency community depends on maintaining consistency in the use of capitalization. Accurate valuation, transactional, and analytical discussions are ensured by accurate usage of Bitcoin and bitcoin. Following these standards improves clarity and gets rid of uncertainty in conversations about cryptocurrencies.

Despite having identical names, Bitcoin and bitcoin both have unique meanings and roles within the cryptocurrency ecosystem. The groundbreaking decentralized cryptocurrency system known simply as "Bitcoin," with a capital "B," has changed the financial industry. It functions as a form of virtual currency and as a representation of the larger cryptocurrency movement. The lowest unit of account within the Bitcoin system, bitcoin, denoted by a lowercase "b," is used to enable accurate transactions and valuations. To properly navigate the cryptocurrency ecosystem and participate in meaningful discussions regarding the technology, financial implications, and future developments, it is essential to understand the differences between these terms. People may speak accurately and confidently in the fascinating realm of cryptocurrencies by making the definitions and capitalization rules clear.

Transaction verification and block addition to the blockchain
The emergence of blockchain technology has fundamentally changed how we transact and store data. Two fundamental operations—transaction verification and blockchain block

addition—are at the heart of this system. These procedures guarantee the decentralized network's safety, transparency, and reliability. This section explores the relevance, processes, and implications of transaction verification and block addition in detail. People may comprehend the core workings of blockchain technology and its potential to transform industries by comprehending these basic procedures.

Blockchain is a distributed and decentralized ledger that keeps track of transactions between a number of nodes, or groups of computers. Consensus, transparency, and immutability are among its core principles. The blockchain is created by grouping each transaction into a block and adding that block to a chain of blocks.

By generating an immutable digital ledger, blockchain technology makes it possible to record transactions in a secure and transparent manner. Because it is decentralized, there is no longer a need for intermediaries, which increases transaction efficiency and lowers costs. The blockchain's public accessibility, which enables anybody to verify and audit transactions, promotes transparency. Once a transaction is added to the blockchain, immutability assures that it cannot be changed or removed without agreement from the network's users.

Consensus-based mechanisms are essential for preserving the reliability and security of the blockchain network. These techniques are in charge of bringing the network nodes to consensus regarding the legitimacy of transactions. Proof-of-Work (PoW) and Proof-of-Stake (PoS) are two popular consensus mechanisms. PoS relies on the ownership of a specific stake in the network to validate transactions, whereas PoW requires users, known as miners, to solve challenging mathematical puzzles.

Before a transaction is added to the blockchain, it must first undergo transaction verification, which is a crucial procedure. Verification makes ensuring that only honest transactions are noted, preventing dishonest or malicious activities.

The integrity of the blockchain must be maintained at all times through transaction verification. The network ensures that only genuine transactions are logged by verifying them, preventing the inclusion of erroneous or malicious transactions. This procedure ensures the accuracy of the recorded information and promotes trust among network users.

Blockchain transactions are signed using individual digital signatures created by cryptographic algorithms. These signatures confirm the sender's identity, guaranteeing that the transaction came from its legitimate source and remaining tamper-proof during transmission. Digital signatures also offer a way to check the transaction's integrity by making sure it hasn't been changed.

Each transaction is verified by nodes inside the blockchain network by looking at the digital signatures, confirming that there are enough funds available, and ensuring that set rules and procedures are being followed. Maintaining the blockchain's security and integrity depends on this validation procedure.

Consensus among the network nodes is necessary for a transaction to be regarded as legitimate. Consensus mechanisms like PoW or PoS ensure that the nodes agree on the transaction's legitimacy. A single node cannot alter the blockchain or add false transactions due to consensus mechanisms. The network ensures that transactions are validated and authorized by a majority of the participants by attaining consensus.

Verified transactions are compiled into blocks and then added to the blockchain through the process of block addition. The chronological order of transactions and the general integrity of the blockchain are preserved through blocks, which operate as storage containers for transactions.

A fundamental procedure that guarantees the blockchain's continuity and security is block adding. Blocks made up of verified transactions are assembled and then uploaded to the blockchain. Transactions are stored in blocks, which provide a timeline of all validated transactions.

The network's valid transactions are gathered and arranged into blocks. The particular blockchain protocol determines the block's size and the number of transactions it can support. Transactions are chosen based on a variety of criteria, including priority, transaction fees, and chronological order.

In PoW-based blockchains, miners compete to find a nonce that satisfies a set of requirements by working through challenging mathematical puzzles. This procedure uses a significant amount of computer resources and serves as a defense against malicious activities. By examining the digital signatures of the transactions, confirming that there are enough funds available, and confirming that the network's rules have been followed, miners validate the transactions contained in the block.

A continuous chain of blocks is created once the block has been verified and added to the current blockchain. The recently added block is connected to the prior block using cryptographic hashes, further securing the blockchain's immutability and transparency. The ledger's state must be updated to reflect the new transactions as part of the block's entry to the blockchain.

The methods for transaction verification and block addition offer a number of benefits that improve the security, transparency, and trustworthiness of the blockchain.

Only genuine and legitimate transactions are added to the blockchain as a result of transaction verification. The blockchain network's consensus mechanisms, such as PoW or PoS, ensure that the majority of users agree that transactions are genuine. The decentralized and consensus-driven nature of the network makes it very impossible for malicious actors to change or tamper with the recorded transactions once a block is added to the blockchain, maintaining the security and immutability of the blockchain.

Due to its openness and accessibility, blockchain technology provides transparency and auditability. Any user of the network has access to the blockchain's data and may check the legitimacy and veracity of any transactions that have been recorded. The capacity for people and organizations to independently audit and verify transactional information increases confidence and accountability within industries that use blockchain technology.

Blockchain technology's decentralized structure eliminates the need for intermediaries and centralized authorities in transactions. Consensus-driven block addition and verification methods guarantee that several network nodes agree on the legitimacy of transactions, improving trust and reducing reliance on a single authority. Decentralization boosts productivity, lowers expenses, and increases resistance to attacks and systemic failures.

The blockchain's overall integrity and dependability are boosted by the block adding and transaction verification processes. A high level of data integrity is provided by the cryptographic techniques employed in digital signatures and consensus mechanisms, ensuring the accuracy and immutability of the recorded transactions. The blockchain's immutability further ensures the accuracy and durability of the data that has been recorded.

While transaction verification and block addition procedures have many benefits, there are also some drawbacks and need for improvement.

Scalability is becoming a major issue as blockchain technology continues to gain popularity and adoption. The verification and block addition processes require computational resources, which may potentially limit the speed at which blockchain networks can operate as well as their capacity. To overcome these difficulties and enable better throughput as well as faster transaction processing, researchers and developers are studying alternative scaling options, including as sharding and layer-two protocols.

Concerns pertaining to the environmental impact of blockchain technology are raised by the fact that consensus mechanisms, particularly PoW, can be energy-intensive. Alternative consensus mechanisms, like PoS or delegated proof-of-stake (DPoS), are being developed in an effort to preserve the security and integrity of the blockchain while consuming less energy.

For blockchain technology to be widely used, it is essential to establish industry-wide standards and achieve interoperability between various blockchain networks. There are initiatives underway to create frameworks and protocols that enable smooth communication and cooperation between various blockchain systems. Interoperability will make it possible to transfer assets and data between other blockchains, increasing the technology's overall usefulness and worth.

Although blockchain technology promotes transparency, it must be balanced with needs for privacy and confidentiality. There are a number of methods being investigated to increase privacy on the blockchain without compromising security and integrity, including zero-knowledge proofs and private transactions.

Blockchain technology relies heavily on the procedures of transaction verification and block addition to guarantee the security, transparency, and reliability of transactions recorded on the blockchain. Transactions are validated through verification, confirming their legitimacy and adherence to predetermined criteria. Block addition generates an unchangeable record of transactions, resulting in a chain of transactions that forms the basis of the blockchain. These procedures disrupt conventional systems and promote innovation by enabling trust, decentralization, and transparency in a variety of industries. For blockchain technology to reach its full potential and achieve widespread use in the future, it will be essential to address issues with scalability, energy consumption, interoperability, and privacy. The future of digital transactions is still being shaped through transaction verification and block addition, fostering a new paradigm of efficiency and trust.

Mining: What it is and how it works

A new era of decentralized digital transactions has begun due to blockchain technology, and mining is at the core of this groundbreaking innovation. The integrity, security, and consensus of the blockchain network are crucially dependent on mining. This section offers a thorough investigation into mining, focusing on its definition, principles, and effects. People can appreciate mining's importance in the blockchain ecosystem and its potential to revolutionize numerous industries by comprehending the complexities of mining.

The computational process of validating and adding new blocks of transactions to the blockchain is referred to as mining. In addition to creating blocks and verifying transactions, it also keeps the decentralized network's security and consensus in tact. In order to safeguard the network and earn rewards, miners compete to solve challenging mathematical puzzles using powerful hardware and specialized software.

The first and most well-known cryptocurrency, Bitcoin, is where the idea of mining first emerged. Individual users may initially access mining with simple computer hardware. However, mining has grown more difficult and resource-intensive as blockchain technology advanced and gained popularity. To accommodate the increasing computing demands of mining, specialized mining gear, such as application-specific integrated circuits (ASICs), emerged.

The consensus mechanisms used by different blockchains are intimately related to mining. Proof-of-Work (PoW) and Proof-of-Stake (PoS) are two often employed techniques.

Blockchains that use Proof-of-Work (PoW) need miners to compete to solve difficult mathematical puzzles called hash functions in order to validate transactions and add new blocks. Miners are required to locate a certain hash value that meets the specified requirements, which demands a significant amount of processing power. The first miner to finish the challenge is granted permission to add a new block to the blockchain and is rewarded with bitcoin.

On the other hand, Proof-of-Stake (PoS) systems select block creators based on their ownership stake in the network. PoS-based systems take into account the cryptocurrency holdings of the participants rather than depending just on processing power. Block makers are selected in a deterministic manner, with the likelihood of selection directly correlated with their stake in the network.

By confirming their authenticity and making sure they adhere to the blockchain network's predefined regulations, miners validate transactions. As part of this verification procedure, the digital signatures are examined, the availability of sufficient funds is verified, and protocol-specific requirements are followed.

After a group of transactions have been validated, miners compile them into a block and add other information, such a timestamp and a reference to the block before it. The block is then transmitted over the network so that other nodes can validate it.

Blockchain protocols modify the mining difficulty in order to maintain a constant block creation rate and regulate the issuance of new currency. The amount of processing required to find a legitimate block hash depends on its difficulty. In order to successfully mine a block, miners must first meet the target value, which is determined by the difficulty. The difficulty adjusts in response to changes in the processing capacity of the network to maintain a roughly constant block production time.

For their efforts in protecting the network and generating new blocks, miners get paid. Newly created bitcoin and transaction fees paid by users for having their transactions included in the block are the usual components of block rewards. For instance, the block reward in Bitcoin started off at 50 bitcoins per block and is half roughly every four years. The controlled issuance of new coins is ensured by this diminishing reward system.

The mining industry has become more competitive in recent years, making it difficult for individual miners to compete against large-scale operations. In order to increase their chances of winning rewards, multiple miners pool their computational power in mining pools. Based on each miner's contribution to the computation, the pools distribute the rewards proportionately among the participating miners.

In order to keep the blockchain's decentralized nature, mining is essential. Mining distributes control and decision-making ability among numerous organizations by providing incentives for players to contribute computational resources. By guaranteeing that no single entity can control the blockchain, the consensus mechanism raises the network's security and trust.

By ensuring transaction validation and verification through mining, double-spending and other fraudulent behaviors are avoided. Any participant can confirm the legitimacy and integrity of transactions recorded in the blocks because of the blockchain's transparency. The promotion of trust, accountability, and auditability within blockchain-using industries is made possible by this transparency.

The blockchain network's resiliency and stability are enhanced through the decentralized mining process. In order for the consensus mechanism to work, a majority of participants must agree that a block is valid. Distributed miners ensure that the network can withstand attacks or failures. Blockchain networks are resistant to censorship, hacking, and single points of failure because of their resilience.

Mining requires significant processing resources, especially in blockchains with a PoW model. Concerns have been expressed regarding how this would affect mining operations' sustainability and the environment. There are currently initiatives to investigate more energy-efficient consensus techniques, such as PoS, that can preserve network security while consuming less energy.

There is a possibility that mining will become more centralized, with a small number of strong entities holding a sizable amount of the mining power, as it grows more competitive and resource-intensive. The blockchain's characteristic decentralization could be compromised if this power concentration continues. Future mining innovations will still face difficulties in striking a balance between decentralization and efficiency.

A significant challenge for mining is scaling blockchain networks to handle an increase in the number of transactions. Congestion and extended confirmation times may result from an increase in transaction volume. Blockchain networks' scalability issues are being addressed by innovations like sharding and layer-two solutions.

Blockchain technology's essential mechanism, mining, permits block formation, transaction verification, and network security. Through computational power and consensus mechanisms, miners compete to create new blocks and validate transactions. The procedure guarantees the blockchain's decentralization, security, and transparency. Addressing issues with energy consumption, centralization, and scalability as blockchain technology develops will open the door for more productive and environmentally friendly mining methods. With its incentive-based approach, mining has the power to transform entire industries, redefine trust models, and reshape the way that transactions and digital economies will be conducted in the future. Mining continues to influence the landscape of decentralized systems because of its crucial position in blockchain technology, opening up new opportunities for a more secure and transparent digital future.

Transaction fees and block rewards

With the introduction of blockchain technology, decentralized digital transactions have taken on a new paradigm where transaction fees and block rewards are crucial in motivating participants and maintaining the network's smooth operation. The purpose of this section is to investigate the mechanics and importance of transaction fees and block rewards in blockchain technology. People can learn more about how blockchain networks achieve security, sustainability, and fairness by exploring the economic implications of these incentives.

Users must pay transaction fees to have their transactions included to the blockchain, which provides miners with a financial incentive to prioritize and approve transactions. These fees compensate miners for the processing power, labor, and time they expended to protect and maintain the blockchain network. Transaction fees are influenced by a number of variables, such as network congestion and transaction size. Users strive to get their transactions validated quickly when network congestion rises, creating a higher fee market. Higher fees are the result of larger transactions using more blockchain space and needing greater computational resources. Transaction fees are determined by the dynamics of supply and demand. Users independently determine the fees they want to pay, and miners decide which transactions to include in a block based on their potential for profit. To increase their earnings, miners often give priority to transactions with higher fees. Longer confirmation periods may be experienced by users who give smaller fees.

Block rewards are incentives given to miners in the form of cryptocurrencies after they successfully add a new block to the blockchain. They act as the main method for issuing new coins and encourage miners to devote computational power to network security. In the Bitcoin network, where the block reward began at 50 bitcoins per block and is halved roughly every four years, the evolution of block rewards may be seen. This decreasing reward mechanism limits the cryptocurrency's overall supply and gradually makes it scarcer. Block rewards give miners compensation for their work, pay for running costs, and give them a financial incentive to keep the network safe. Miners would be less inclined to contribute computational power without block incentives, thus reducing the network's security. Transaction fees become more significant as a cryptocurrency's total supply gets closer to its predetermined limit. Instead of block rewards, transaction fees are anticipated to take over as the main source of miner incentives. This change supports blockchain ecosystems that are viable and profitable.

Significant concerns for network security, decentralization, user experience, and economic sustainability arise from transaction fees and block rewards. They provide miners with incentives for taking part in the consensus mechanism and providing computational power to protect the blockchain network. Robust fee markets and reasonable block rewards guarantee a diverse and decentralized mining ecosystem, lowering the possibility of one organization gaining excessive control over the network. Transaction fees have a direct impact on how quickly transactions are confirmed; larger fees result in quicker settlements. Users looking to complete transactions quickly may decide to charge greater fees. It becomes crucial for users to balance the desired confirmation time with a reasonable charge. The economic viability of blockchain networks is further aided by transaction costs and block rewards. Transaction fees balance the cost of participation with the value gained from the network by encouraging users to pay for the resources they utilize. A sustainable mining ecosystem is promoted by properly calibrated block rewards, which make sure that miners are fairly compensated for their work.

For blockchain networks, scalability and fee market effectiveness are challenges. Congestion can result in increased transaction costs and longer confirmation times as popularity increases. These issues can be resolved and fee market efficiency can be improved by creating effective scaling solutions, such as layer-two protocols or sharding. For enhancing user experience, user education and fee optimization are essential. Individuals can be empowered to optimize their transaction fees and strike a balance between price and speed by being given access to user-friendly fee estimation tools and educational resources. Stability in the fee market is also an issue because volatility can affect users' perceptions of the network and their trust in it. Techniques including fee estimating models, fee caps, and fee market algorithms can help create a more stable fee market environment by lowering volatility and improving user experience.

Blockchain economics must include transaction fees and block rewards. Transaction fees compensate miners for their computational resources and encourage prompt transaction validation. The blockchain network's security and long-term viability are guaranteed by block rewards. For network security, user satisfaction, and long-term economic viability, a balance between transaction fees and block rewards is crucial. As blockchain technology develops, overcoming scalability issues and maximizing fee market effectiveness will be crucial to building strong and user-friendly blockchain ecosystems. Individuals can navigate the blockchain ecosystem by understanding the economics underpinning transaction fees and block rewards, which unlocks the potential for secure, decentralized, and financially sustainable digital transactions.

CHAPTER
IV
Wallets, Addresses, and Keys

What is a Bitcoin wallet?

Digital transactions have undergone a revolution due to Bitcoin, the pioneering cryptocurrency. The Bitcoin wallet, a crucial tool that enables users to safely store, manage, and conduct transactions with their digital assets, lies at the center of this decentralized ecosystem. This section aims to provide a thorough grasp of what a Bitcoin wallet is by examining its features, classifications, security precautions, and the shifting technological landscape of wallets. People may navigate the world of digital assets with security and confidence by learning the nuances of Bitcoin wallets.

A Bitcoin wallet is a piece of hardware or software that enables users to store, control, and communicate with their Bitcoin holdings. The cryptographic keys needed to access and transmit Bitcoin are safely stored by it. Key pair generation, transaction management, security, and authentication are just a few of the roles that Bitcoin wallets perform. A public key and a private key are created during key pair generation. While the private key is kept private and is used to access and approve Bitcoin transactions, the public key serves as the user's wallet address. Users can transfer and receive Bitcoin through transaction management, view transaction history, and keep track of wallet balances. Users' private keys are protected by security and authentication procedures, which use encryption, password security, and multi-factor authentication to assure only allowed access.

There are many different types of bitcoin wallets, each with unique features and levels of protection. Software wallets, hardware wallets, and paper wallets are the three most popular varieties. Software wallets include mobile wallets, which are created for smartphones to give ease and portability, as well as desktop wallets, which are installed on PCs and allow complete management and protection. Web wallets are convenient but rely on the security precautions taken by the wallet provider. They are accessed using web browsers. Hardware wallets, which are physical items, offer higher security by keeping private keys offline. Paper wallets provide an offline and inexpensive storage solution by physically printing or writing down private and public keys on paper.

When it comes to Bitcoin wallets, security is of the utmost significance. It is essential to preserve private keys, and encryption methods are used to keep keys protected from unauthorized access. The usage of strong, original passwords is encouraged since password protection adds an additional layer of security. By requiring a second form of identification, such as a fingerprint or one-time password, multi-factor authentication increases wallet security. Data loss or device failure is protected by backup and recovery procedures, and it is advised to periodically backup wallet data in a safe offline or cloud storage location. The security and integrity of Bitcoin assets are ensured by picking a trusted wallet service.

With the development of technology, Bitcoin wallets continue to change. Multiple private key signatures are required by multi-signature wallets in order to approve a transaction, offering an extra layer of security and lowering the possibility of compromised keys. In order to ensure simplicity of use and effective backup and recovery procedures, hierarchical deterministic (HD) wallets generate a hierarchy of keys from a single master seed. Coin mixing, stealth addresses, and secret transactions are just a few of the features that privacy-focused wallets provide to increase the anonymity and fungibility of Bitcoin transactions.

Tools for securely managing, storing, and using Bitcoin include Bitcoin wallets. They allow for seamless communication with the

Bitcoin network and provide users control over their private keys. People can make educated decisions and protect their digital assets by being aware of the many types of wallets, the security issues they raise, and the changing landscape of wallet technology. By adopting safe wallet procedures, people may navigate the Bitcoin universe with confidence and make use of this groundbreaking technology's potential. Wallet technology will be essential in determining the security, usability, and user experience of the digital asset space as the Bitcoin ecosystem develops further. Individuals can participate in the world of Bitcoin with confidence and protect their digital assets by adopting secure wallet practices.

Public and private keys: An overview

Within the realm of modern cryptography, the concept of public and private keys serves as an essential component in the process of ensuring the safety of digital transactions and communications. Encryption, decryption, and the validation of digital signatures are all made possible by using these keys in conjunction with one another within a cryptographic system. The purpose of this sectionis to provide a comprehensive review of public and private keys by examining their definitions, functions, the underlying mathematics that makes them secure, as well as their applications in a variety of different domains. Individuals can gain a better understanding of the significance of cryptographic security in the digital era and the consequences it has for the safety of data, the confidentiality of digital communication, and the trustworthiness of digital transactions by delving deeper into the complexities of public and private keys.

Symmetric and asymmetric cryptography are the two main classifications that can be applied to cryptographic systems. When it comes to encryption and decryption, symmetric cryptography only uses a single key, while asymmetric cryptography, which makes use of both public and private keys, is able to overcome the difficulties associated with a safe key exchange.

The employment of a public key and a private key is essential to the practice of public key cryptography, which is also known as asymmetric cryptography. Anyone can verify digital signatures or encrypt data because the public key is freely distributed and available to the public. The private key can be used for both decryption and signing, but it must always be kept confidential. Complex mathematical techniques based on prime numbers and modular arithmetic are used to generate the pair of keys needed to access the system.

The practice of using a single private key for both encryption and decryption is at the heart of private key cryptography, which is also known by the name symmetric cryptography. Its primary application is in symmetric encryption methods, which encrypt and decrypt data using the same key in both processes.

Both public and private keys are useful for a variety of purposes and can be put to use in a number of contexts.

The use of public keys in cryptography makes secure communication possible by offering both confidentiality and privacy. When a communication is encrypted by the sender using the recipient's public key, the sender ensures that only the recipient, who possesses the corresponding private key, is able to decrypt the message and access the message's original content. During the transmission procedure, sensitive information is shielded by this method.

The use of public key cryptography is very necessary in order to validate the authenticity and integrity of digital signatures. The sender generates an unique digital signature by signing a message with their own personal private key. Verifying the signature and ensuring that the message has not been altered while in transit can both be accomplished with the help of the sender's public key, which is available to the recipient. The verification of document integrity, authentication, and non-repudiation are all significantly aided by the use of digital signatures.

The use of public keys in cryptography makes it possible to exchange keys in a secure manner. It is possible for two parties to establish a shared secret key through the use of methods such as the Diffie-Hellman key exchange without directly exchanging the key itself. This procedure ensures that all communications are protected and that all data transmissions are encrypted.

The integrity of public and private key cryptography is dependent not only on the length and strength of the keys, but also on the management of the keys in an appropriate manner.

The length of the key and the difficulty of the mathematical procedures that are used to generate it are two factors that determine how secure public- and private-key cryptography is. Longer key lengths offer improved resistance against brute-force assaults, which makes it computationally impossible to crack the encryption by trying all possible key combinations.

It is absolutely necessary to have effective key management in order to keep both public and private keys secure. It is essential to safely preserve private keys and prevent unwanted access to them at all times. For the sake of maintaining both authenticity and integrity, public keys should only be disseminated through reliable methods.

Both public and private keys have their uses in a variety of fields, including the development of secure communication protocols such as HTTPS, SSH, and VPNs. In legal contracts, financial transactions, and electronic voting systems, they are essential for verifying the document's integrity, authenticating the document, and ensuring that the document cannot be repudiated. In addition, public key cryptography makes it possible to have safe key exchange procedures, which makes it possible to send data in an encrypted form.

Modern cryptographic systems are built on a foundation of public and private keys, which are responsible for enabling secure communication, maintaining the integrity of data, and building trust in digital transactions. In this day and age, where data security is of the utmost importance, it is important that you have a fundamental understanding of the principles and operations underlying these keys. Individuals and organizations are able to protect sensitive information, establish secure communication channels, and foster trust in the digital arena when they apply correct key management policies and leverage the power of public and private keys. In the constantly shifting environment of technology and data protection, cryptographic security that is based on public and private keys will continue to be a vital component.

Bitcoin addresses: Creation and usage

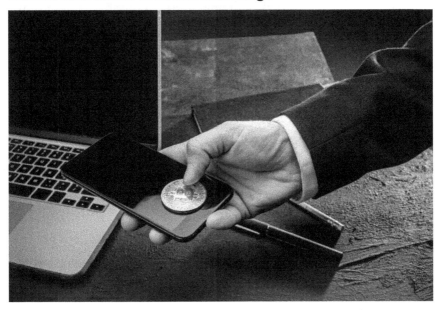

The ground-breaking digital currency Bitcoin uses a decentralized network and individual addresses to carry out transactions. As identifiers for sending and receiving funds, bitcoin addresses uphold the system's security and transparency. The goal of this section is to give readers a thorough grasp of Bitcoin addresses by exploring their creation, structure, and actual application in transactional contexts. Individuals may successfully and clearly navigate the realm of digital finance by learning about the complexities of Bitcoin addresses.

Alphanumeric strings known as bitcoin addresses identify the source or destination of funds on the Bitcoin network. They serve as public identities and make it possible for people to securely and openly accept money from others. Bitcoin addresses are necessary for confirming a specific account's transaction history and balance.

An average Bitcoin address includes a version number, a hash of the public key, and a checksum. The format is often a string of alphanumeric characters, frequently starting with "1" for regular addresses and "3" for multi-signature addresses.

Bitcoin addresses come in a variety of formats, including Pay-to-Public-Key-Hash (P2PKH), Pay-to-Script-Hash (P2SH), and Bech32. Each type offers distinctive characteristics and is compatible with various wallet platforms.

The private key and the public key of a cryptographic key pair are used to create Bitcoin addresses. The owner's secret is the private key, which is produced at random. From the private key, a corresponding public key is mathematically derived.

The public key is hashed to produce a Bitcoin address, often using the SHA-256 and RIPEMD-160 algorithms. A fixed-length string that accurately represents the public key is created as a result of this process—the public key hash.

A version number is added to the public key hash to distinguish between various address formats. Additionally, a checksum is created by hashing the version number and public key hash, and a portion of the resulting hash is appended to the address. When manually inputting addresses, the checksum ensures accuracy and prevents typical mistakes.

Base58 encoding is used to show the address in a more accessible format, excluding ambiguous characters like "0," "O," "I," and "l." The address is less susceptible to transcription errors due to this encoding, which converts the hash data into a series of alphanumeric characters.

Bitcoin addresses are mostly used to receive money. When someone wants to receive bitcoin, they give the sender their specific address. Anyone can view the amount and transaction history related to that address because to the blockchain's transparency.

The recipient's Bitcoin address must be specified as the destination when transferring Bitcoin. The recipient's address is used by the sender's wallet to build a transaction, which is then digitally signed with the sender's private key. After being broadcast to the network, the transaction is then verified and added to the blockchain.

The single-use nature of Bitcoin addresses encourages privacy and security. Reusing addresses makes it possible for outsiders to connect numerous transactions to a single entity, which compromises anonymity. To protect privacy and reduce the possibility of address-based analysis, it is advised to produce a new address for each transaction.

A further level of convenience and security is provided by hierarchical deterministic (HD) wallets. Users can deterministically generate an infinite number of addresses because they produce a hierarchical tree-like structure of addresses from a single master seed. HD wallets enable secure backup and recovery procedures easier and simplify key administration.

Protecting the accompanying private keys is essential for maintaining the security of Bitcoin addresses. To protect their private keys from loss or unwanted access, users must use secure storage methods like hardware wallets or encrypted digital wallets.

It is essential to routinely backup private keys or use wallet backup features to reduce the risk of losing access to funds. Backup copies should be encrypted or safely stored offline.

It is crucial to confirm the accuracy of the address provided by the sender before accepting any Bitcoin. Address tampering that is unintentional or deliberate can be avoided by checking the first and final few characters, employing QR codes, or depending on trustworthy payment request methods.

In the ecosystem of digital currencies, Bitcoin addresses are essential for facilitating secure and open transactions. Individuals are able to confidently participate in the world of digital banking when they understand the formation process, structure, and practical application of Bitcoin addresses. Users can make sure that Bitcoin addresses are used securely and responsibly by putting a priority on issues like private key protection, address verification, and privacy considerations. Addressing improvements and innovations will improve the effectiveness, security, and privacy of digital transactions as the Bitcoin network continues to develop. Individuals can unlock the full potential of this groundbreaking technology by adopting the core ideas and procedures governing Bitcoin addresses.

Wallet types: Hot wallets, cold wallets, hardware wallets, paper wallets

The idea of wallets is fundamental in the world of cryptocurrencies for storing and safeguarding digital assets. Wallets are hardware or software devices that let users transmit, receive, and store cryptocurrencies like Bitcoin. This section explores the various wallet varieties, including paper wallets, hardware wallets, hot wallets, and cold wallets. People who are knowledgeable about the features, benefits, and vulnerabilities of each type of wallet can decide how to best protect their digital assets.

Digital wallets known as "hot wallets," which are online-connected and give users rapid access to their cryptocurrency holdings. They are available in a variety of formats, including web-based wallets offered by outside service providers and software-based wallets like desktop and mobile wallets. Hot wallets' main objective is to give customers effective control over their cryptocurrency funds.

Users have instant access to sending and receiving cryptocurrency due to hot wallets. They provide simple user interfaces that make cryptocurrency network transactions easy. Hot wallets enable users to easily keep track of their holdings and carry out transactions with features like balance monitoring, transaction history, and address management.

Hot wallets may be practical, but it's important to be aware of their security risks as well. Users of hot wallets need to be aware of the vulnerabilities that being online exposes them to.

Hot wallets are significantly at risk from online threats. To access funds without authorization, hackers may attack web-based systems or take advantage of vulnerabilities in software wallets. Users must take precautions to avoid common threats like malware and phishing attacks. Additionally, some hot wallets are run by third-party service providers, necessitating that users have trust in the security measures taken by these organizations.

Users can put numerous security measures into place to lessen the security risks related to hot wallets. When used in conjunction with a password, two-factor authentication (2FA) offers an additional layer of security. The wallet and private keys are encrypted to help prevent unauthorized access. The wallet software is regularly patched and updated to make sure that any known vulnerabilities are quickly fixed. To reduce the risk of utilizing compromised wallet software, it's also crucial to get hot wallets from reliable sources.

Hot wallets are practical, but it's important to understand the risks that they pose. Users must be on the lookout for malware, phishing scams, and other online risks that could compromise the security of their hot wallets. Securing cryptocurrency holdings requires raising awareness of potential risks and promoting education about them.

Hot wallets are ideal for people that frequently transact in cryptocurrencies or need quick access to their money. Hot wallets' simplicity and effectiveness are advantageous to traders, active users, and anyone who frequently utilize cryptocurrencies for payment.

It is advised that users think about risk management and wallet diversity. Risks related to holding all of your assets in one hot wallet can be reduced by distributing your money across several wallets. A further degree of security can be added by putting the majority of your cryptocurrency holdings in cold wallets or hardware wallets and allocating a tiny amount to a hot wallet for daily use.

It is essential to find trustworthy wallet providers with a track record of security and customer satisfaction when choosing hot wallets. To guarantee the wallet provider's credibility and dependability, in-depth investigation and due diligence are important.

When using hot wallets, it's crucial to evaluate your risk tolerance. Users should assess how much cryptocurrency they plan to put in a hot wallet and take into account the possibility of loss. Smaller quantities should normally be kept in hot wallets, while larger amounts should be kept in more safe storage.

Hot wallets provide users with accessibility and ease when handling their cryptocurrency funds. Despite the fact that they offer immediate access and user-friendly interfaces, it is crucial to take into account the security threats brought on by their online nature. The best way to ensure the security of cryptocurrency holdings is to implement strong security measures, keep up with the most recent cybersecurity trends, and use hot wallets with caution. Users can make use of the advantages of hot wallets while reducing potential hazards by using risk management measures, diversifying their wallets, and selecting reputable providers. Individuals are better equipped to make educated decisions and confidently participate in the realm of digital banking when they understand the functionality and security implications of hot wallets.

Cold wallets are intended for managing cryptocurrency funds offline while storing private keys. Cold wallets make sure that private keys are never exposed to online risks, in contrast to hot wallets that are connected to the internet. They come in a variety of forms, the most popular being hardware wallets and paper wallets.

Hardware wallets are physical items made for the purpose of safely storing offline private keys. They are extremely safe because they frequently use robust encryption and demand physical confirmation of transactions. On the other hand, paper wallets generate and print private keys on physical things like paper. They offer an additional layer of protection and are fully offline.

Cold wallets' defense against online dangers is one of its main benefits. Private keys are protected from hacking attempts and malware since they are never made available online, unlike hot wallets. Cold wallets also reduce the chance of falling prey to phishing scams that seek for customers' private data. In addition to providing physical security, cold wallets offer protection against online dangers. They reduce the possibility of physical loss or unauthorized access to cryptocurrency holdings by keeping private keys offline. To make sure that only authorized users can access the funds, several hardware wallets incorporate additional security features like multi-factor authentication or password-protected access. Additionally, the majority of cold wallets offer tools for safely backing up and recovering wallets, enabling users to get their funds back in case their device is misplaced, broken, or stolen.

Cold wallets are ideal for storing cryptocurrency assets over an extended period of time. People who keep a sizable percentage of their money in cold wallets can benefit from increased security against potential threats. These wallets can create signed transaction data that may then be broadcast to the network when the wallet is linked to an online device, making them usable even for offline transactions. This function makes it possible to conduct secure transactions even when there is little to no internet connectivity.

Diversifying wallet use is advised in order to find a balance between convenience and security. While the majority of the funds can be kept in cold wallets for long-term safekeeping, hot wallets can be utilized for everyday transactions. Cold wallets should routinely receive firmware updates to guarantee they have the most recent security features and bug fixes. Keeping up with recommended procedures, such as safely maintaining backup copies of private keys, offers an additional layer of security.

A strong and safe way to store cryptocurrency offline, cold wallets offer defense against online threats and physical theft. One way for people to protect their digital assets is to keep their private keys offline. Cold wallets offer consumers increase their level of security and peace of mind when protecting their cryptocurrency investments, whether through hardware wallets or paper wallets. People can increase the security of their cryptocurrency storage by using multiple wallets, staying up to date with firmware updates, and following best practices. People can make well-informed judgments and strengthen their bitcoin storage practices by being aware of the cold wallet's features and security considerations.

Hardware wallets are physical items created for managing cryptocurrency funds and securely storing private keys. They provide an offline setting, guaranteeing that private keys are shielded from any dangers online. There are many different types of hardware wallets, including smartcards, USB-based devices, and specialized equipment. They use innovative encryption techniques and security features to keep private keys safe from unauthorized access. Hardware wallets give the highest level of security compared to other wallet types because they offer offline storage.

Hardware wallets come with a number of security benefits. They first offer offline storage, removing the threat of malware, phishing, and other online threats. Second, to guard against physical theft or manipulation of private keys, hardware wallets frequently include secure components like tamper-resistant circuits. They also add an additional layer of security by requiring a special PIN number to access and manage cryptocurrency funds. Last but not least, hardware wallets frequently have built-in screens that enable users confirm and authorize transactions right on the device, reducing the possibility of transaction tampering.

User-friendliness is prioritized in hardware wallets, making them usable even by those with a basic understanding of technology. The interfaces make it easier to create addresses, manage cryptocurrency assets, and confirm transactions. Through the use of intuitive button configurations, users are able to swiftly navigate through the available menu options, view their account balances, and begin conducting transactions.

Numerous cryptocurrencies are supported by hardware wallets, allowing users to store and control various digital assets at once. They are a flexible storage option for a range of cryptocurrency portfolios because of their compatibility. A hardware wallet's unified interface allows users to easily handle a variety of coins and tokens, reducing the process of managing cryptocurrencies.

Hardware wallets' resilience to online threats is one of their main benefits. They eliminate the possibility of hacking, malware assaults, and phishing efforts by keeping private keys offline. Regular firmware upgrades for hardware wallets also assist the devices by addressing possible vulnerabilities and ensuring that they have the most recent security features and bug fixes. Users should only buy hardware wallets from trusted vendors, and they should confirm the devices' legitimacy, in order to maximize security.

Hardware wallets offer rigorous physical security features in addition to online protection. To prevent physical tampering or the extraction of private keys, these devices use tamper-resistant features, such as anti-tamper coatings, seals, and secure parts. Even in the case of device loss or theft, users can make sure that their private keys are protected.

Although hardware wallets offer strong protection, users must take care to keep their devices secure. This includes safely keeping the hardware wallet's backup seeds or recovery phrases, which are necessary for wallet recovery. Additionally, users should update their firmware regularly to take advantage of the most recent security upgrades made available by the hardware wallet's maker. To minimize the risk of utilizing compromised or counterfeit devices, it is crucial to confirm the hardware wallet's legitimacy before use.

For the long-term safekeeping of cryptocurrency assets, particularly sizable amounts that are not frequently accessed, hardware wallets are ideal. Individuals can gain from improved security against potential threats by putting a sizable amount of their funds in hardware wallets. Since these wallets enable users to create signed transaction data, which can then be broadcast to the network when the wallet is linked to an internet device, they are also appropriate for offline transactions. For a balance between security and accessibility, it is advised to vary wallet usage by combining hardware wallets with hot wallets. To guarantee that the hardware wallets include the newest security features and bug fixes, regular firmware updates should be installed.

Hardware wallets, which offer offline storage, high-level encryption, and user-friendly interfaces, have become the ideal security companion for cryptocurrency storage. Hardware wallets provide unrivaled protection against internet threats and physical tampering by keeping private keys offline and utilizing strong security protections. To exploit the security advantages provided by hardware wallets, users must follow best practices, such as safely storing backup seeds and often updating firmware. For those looking to protect their cryptocurrency investments, hardware wallets have taken over as the preferred option due to their versatility, simplicity, and unmatched security. Individuals are better equipped to make informed judgments and confidently enter the realm of digital banking when they understand the functionality and security implications of hardware wallets.

Paper wallets are physical documents that have the data needed to store and access cryptocurrency funds without an internet connection. They are made up of printed private keys and public addresses, which are frequently presented as alphanumeric or QR codes. The private keys are never made available to online threats since paper wallets are prepared with offline equipment. They add an additional layer of security by completely keeping digital assets offline.

Paper wallets come with a number of distinctive security benefits. They are resistant to online hacking efforts, viruses, and phishing attacks since they are built and stored offline. The risk of unwanted access to cryptocurrency funds is much reduced because the private keys are never made public on the internet. Paper wallets also do away with the need to depend on unreliable service providers, giving customers direct access to their funds.

Making a paper wallet is simple to do and doesn't require any technological knowledge. Paper wallets can be created using a variety of online tools and applications, enabling users to securely print their private keys and public addresses. Paper wallets are also simple to use because the required data can be saved in physical form and preserved in a secure location.

By keeping the private keys offline, paper wallets offer genuine cold storage capabilities. The risk of online wallet and exchange-related digital vulnerabilities is removed by this offline storage. Users can maximize the security of their cryptocurrency assets by safely storing their paper wallets in physical places like safes or lockboxes.

It is important to work in a safe and reliable setting when making a paper wallet. It is essential to utilize trustworthy offline tools and check the software's reliability. Users are responsible for making sure that their operating system and printer are secure and free of malware. The printed paper wallet's security must also be maintained through careful management, such as guarding it against physical harm or unauthorized access.

Paper wallet duplication is essential for backup and redundancy. Users should think about printing multiple copies of the paper wallet and safely keeping them in various places around their home. This procedure makes sure that there are still backup copies available in case one copy is destroyed, lost, or compromised, allowing for the funds to be recovered.

Paper wallets offer exceptional security, but they also have certain drawbacks. The private keys must be imported into a software or hardware wallet in order to access cryptocurrency funds kept in a paper wallet. Users must comprehend the potential risks and difficulties involved in this procedure, often known as "sweeping" the wallet, and carefully follow it. Given their physical character and the necessity to protect them against damage or loss, paper wallets could not be as portable as other wallet types.

For long-term safekeeping of sizable cryptocurrency assets that are not frequently accessed, paper wallets are excellent. By keeping private keys offline and away from online dangers, they provide the highest level of protection. Users need to make sure they produce paper wallets with reputable offline tools, handle and keep them safely, and make several backups in various physical locations. It is critical to understand the dangers and difficulties involved with importing private keys from a paper wallet and to use caution while accessing funds.

Paper wallets offer bitcoin owners a safe, offline storage option for their digital assets, ensuring their protection. Paper wallets provide security in the cryptocurrency ecosystem due to its unique security advantages, simplicity of creation, and actual cold storage capabilities. To maximize security, users must follow best practices in the creation, management, backup, and procedure of gaining access to funds. People are better equipped to make wise choices and confidently protect their bitcoin investments when they are aware of the functions and security considerations of paper wallets.

CHAPTER
V
Buying, Selling,
and Using Bitcoin

How and where to buy Bitcoin

The pioneering cryptocurrency, Bitcoin, has become incredibly popular in recent years. Understanding the various platforms and techniques for purchasing Bitcoin is crucial for anyone interested in doing so. This section offers a thorough tutorial on where and how to purchase Bitcoin. It examines the many options, including peer-to-peer networks, cryptocurrency exchanges, and Bitcoin ATMs.

People may comfortably navigate the Bitcoin market and make wise judgments if they have a complete understanding of the buying process and the platforms involved.

Online marketplaces called cryptocurrency exchanges make it easier to acquire and sell digital assets like Bitcoin. They offer a simple and convenient means of breaking into the cryptocurrency industry. It's important to select a trustworthy exchange, taking into account aspects like reputation, security precautions, user experience, and accepted payment methods. Before placing a buy order, which can be executed quickly or placed as a limit order, an account must be created and identity verified. Exchanges for cryptocurrencies provide a variety of features and trading alternatives to accommodate different preferences.

Without the assistance of a centralized exchange, buyers and sellers can trade Bitcoin directly using peer-to-peer (P2P) platforms. These platforms provide more flexibility and privacy. Considerations for selecting a trustworthy P2P platform include user reviews, escrow services, dispute resolution procedures, and security measures. Users can register, verify their identification, view listings, and negotiate terms with sellers. In order to arrange payment and the transfer of Bitcoin from escrow to the buyer's wallet, communication is essential.

Physical machines called bitcoin ATMs let consumers buy Bitcoin with cash or a debit or credit card. Online resources that offer thorough maps and directories can be used to locate a Bitcoin ATM. In order to use a Bitcoin ATM, you must first find the closest one, choose the "Buy Bitcoin" option, input the necessary amount, provide a Bitcoin wallet address, and then pay with cash or a credit card. The bought Bitcoin is subsequently sent to the designated wallet.

There are various security considerations and best practices that should be followed to guarantee a risk-free Bitcoin purchasing experience. These include adopting strong passwords, enabling two-factor authentication, and safeguarding personal Bitcoin wallets with reliable providers. Before making a purchase, platforms should be thoroughly investigated in order to find reliable and trustworthy platforms. To take advantage of improved security measures, wallets and trading platforms need to regularly update their software and firmware. Maintaining a secure environment requires ongoing education and keeping up with the most recent security procedures in the bitcoin industry.

It's important to carefully weigh your options when buying Bitcoin and be aware of the procedures involved. Different ways to purchase Bitcoin are available, each with their own advantages and considerations, including peer-to-peer networks, Bitcoin ATMs, and cryptocurrency exchanges. People can confidently enter the world of Bitcoin ownership by picking reliable platforms, finishing required verifications, and implementing best security measures. A safe and satisfying Bitcoin purchase experience depends on staying informed, adjusting to changing security measures, and continuously educating oneself. It's critical to approach Bitcoin purchases with caution, research, and a commitment to personal protection as the cryptocurrency industry continues to develop.

Selling Bitcoin: Platforms and process

The first cryptocurrency, Bitcoin, has become incredibly popular in recent years. Understanding the selling procedure for Bitcoin is essential as more people and companies use this digital asset. This section will examine the platforms and procedures involved in selling Bitcoin in order to help readers make wise judgments and successfully navigate the cryptocurrency market.

Understanding the fundamentals of Bitcoin is crucial before getting started with selling it. Blockchain, a decentralized network that underpins Bitcoin, safely and openly records every transaction. It can be purchased, traded, and exchanged utilizing a variety of channels and marketplaces and only exists in digital form.

The most popular venues for selling Bitcoin are cryptocurrency exchanges. These online marketplaces make it easier to buy and trade Bitcoin and other cryptocurrencies. The well-known exchanges Coinbase, Binance, Kraken, and Bitstamp are just some examples. Considerations for selecting an exchange include its security protocols, fees, liquidity, supported countries, and user-friendliness.

Peer-to-peer (P2P) platforms eliminate the need for an exchange to act as an intermediary by putting buyers and sellers in direct contact. Two well-known P2P platforms are LocalBitcoins and Paxful. They offer a variety of payment alternatives, including bank transfers, cash deposits, and gift cards, and they provide a secure area for people to exchange Bitcoin. In P2P transactions, it is essential to use caution and confirm the legitimacy of the counterparty.

Users normally need to register for an account on the preferred platform in order to sell Bitcoin. This entails supplying personal data, completing identification verification processes, or KYCs, and creating a strong password. Depending on the platform and the jurisdiction, different KYC requirements may apply.

It is vital to have a digital wallet to store and send Bitcoin before selling it. Wallets might be web-based (Coinbase Wallet, MyEtherWallet), software-based (Electrum, Exodus), or hardware-based (Ledger, Trezor). Protecting one's digital assets requires selecting a trustworthy and secure wallet.

The selling process can start after the wallet and account have been created. Users often go to the "Sell" or "Trade" area of a cryptocurrency exchange, choose Bitcoin as the asset, enter the required quantity or price, and then check the transaction's specifics. Sellers can post listings on P2P sites that include the quantity of Bitcoin they are offering for sale, the preferred mode of payment, and any other conditions.

The platform links the seller's offer with potential purchasers after starting the transaction. On exchanges, the transaction takes place on the platform itself, with the exchange serving as an intermediary to speed up the procedure. P2P systems match prospective buyers and sellers, and the discussion and transactional process takes place directly between the parties.

Once a buyer has been identified and a deal has been reached, the buyer uses the preferred method to make the payment. This can involve cash transactions, bank transfers, or online payment systems like PayPal and Venmo. Usually, the seller receives the money directly into their designated wallet or into their account on the platform. Before sending the customer their Bitcoin, it is crucial to confirm that the money has been received.

Selling bitcoin carries the risk of being the target of scams, fraud, and hacker attempts. Users should turn on two-factor authentication (2FA) for their accounts, update their wallet software frequently, and take caution when engaging with strangers to reduce these risks. Using trusted platforms with robust security measures and storing Bitcoin in a secure wallet are essential.

Selling Bitcoin could result in tax obligations, depending on the country. To ensure compliance, it is crucial to speak with tax experts or become familiar with the relevant tax laws. By being aware of the legal implications of cryptocurrency transactions, sellers can steer clear of potential legal problems.

With the ability to exchange digital assets for fiat money or other investments, selling Bitcoin has grown to be a crucial component of the cryptocurrency ecosystem. People can confidently navigate the world of Bitcoin sales by choosing the appropriate platform, comprehending the selling procedure, and putting the essential security measures in place. Making profitable Bitcoin transactions will depend on your ability to stay informed and adjust to changes as the cryptocurrency market develops.

Using Bitcoin for transactions: Where and how?

The first decentralized digital currency in the world, Bitcoin, has shown to be a competitive alternative to established financial institutions. A growing number of people and companies are looking to conduct transactions using Bitcoin as a result of its rising popularity. In order to better understand the where, when, and how of using Bitcoin for transactions, this section will offer details on the platforms, businesses, and procedures involved.

Value is transferred from one Bitcoin address to another during a Bitcoin transaction. The blockchain, a decentralized public ledger that guarantees transparency and immutability, contains records of these transactions. There are inputs (funding sources) and outputs (funding receivers) in every transaction. To fully grasp the complexities of using Bitcoin for transactions, it is essential to comprehend the structure of Bitcoin transactions.

Individuals require a digital wallet that enables them to send and receive Bitcoin in order to utilize Bitcoin for transactions. Unique Bitcoin addresses are created by wallets and serve as places to send and receive funds. Each address is made up of a private key (used for signing transactions) and a public key (address), which together form a cryptographic key pair. Hardware wallets, software wallets, and web-based wallets are just a few of the several types of wallets available.

More online retailers are now accepting Bitcoin as a form of payment. Businesses can take Bitcoin through integrations and plugins from e-commerce platforms like Shopify and WooCommerce. Customers can also use Bitcoin to make online purchases from reputable merchants like Microsoft, Overstock, and Newegg. Payment processors like BitPay and CoinGate help merchants accept Bitcoin payments and, if needed, convert Bitcoin into conventional currencies.

Although it's still uncommon, several physical stores and companies now accept Bitcoin as payment. Restaurants, cafes, bars, and retail stores can advertise Bitcoin payment QR codes or accept payments using dedicated payment terminals. Directories that support Bitcoin, like Coinmap and Airbitz, offer maps and listings of physical businesses that accept Bitcoin.

Buying gift cards or vouchers with Bitcoin is another option to transact with it. A variety of gift cards from well-known retailers are available on websites like eGifter and Gyft, enabling users to indirectly purchase goods and services from those stores using Bitcoin. When a transaction is made, these platforms serve as intermediaries, transforming Bitcoin into gift cards.

People must first create a digital wallet before using Bitcoin for transactions. This entails selecting a wallet type (hardware, software, or web-based), creating an account according to the wallet provider's instructions, and securing the created private key(s). The user-friendly interface that wallets normally offer enables users to monitor their Bitcoin balances, create addresses, and start transactions.

The sender needs the recipient's Bitcoin address in order to complete a Bitcoin transaction. The recipient can send a QR code or a group of alphanumeric characters as their Bitcoin address. The sender enters the recipient's address and the requested Bitcoin amount in the transaction interface of their wallet. Next, a transaction is created by the wallet software, digitally signed with the sender's private key, and broadcast to the Bitcoin network.

A transaction is broadcasted and then enters the mempool of the Bitcoin network to await confirmation. The transaction is added to a block by miners, who protect the network, by resolving challenging mathematical puzzles. The transaction is deemed complete once it has been verified and included in a block. Depending on network congestion, confirmation times vary; often, greater prices lead to faster confirmation.

Transaction fees are a common component of Bitcoin transactions, which motivates miners to quickly include the transaction in a block. Depending on the network's congestion and the intended transaction speed, transaction fees may change. Users can typically select the fee level in digital wallets according on their preferences.

The volatility of the price of Bitcoin makes it difficult to use as a medium of exchange. When transacting with Bitcoin, customers and merchants must be cautious of exchange rate fluctuations. To address this issue, payment processors and wallets frequently offer real-time conversion rates.

When using Bitcoin for transactions, security and privacy must come first. Users should follow recommended practices, including protecting their private keys, using wallets with high levels of security, and being watchful of phishing scams and harmful software. Additionally, since transaction information is viewable on the public blockchain, Bitcoin's pseudonymous nature presents privacy problems.

Different jurisdictions have different regulatory environments governing Bitcoin transactions. To ensure compliance, users should become familiar with the relevant laws and rules, particularly those pertaining to taxation, money transmission, and anti-money laundering procedures.

With its ability to facilitate borderless, secure, and decentralized transactions, Bitcoin has become a disruptive force in the financial industry. People can make use of the advantages of this digital currency by comprehending the fundamentals of Bitcoin transactions, figuring out where Bitcoin is accepted, and taking the necessary procedures to utilize Bitcoin for transactions. Despite difficulties and concerns, the emergence of Bitcoin as a practical payment method is being driven by ongoing adoption and innovation in the Bitcoin community.

CHAPTER
VI
Bitcoin Trading and Investing

Bitcoin as an investment: Pros and cons

The first decentralized cryptocurrency in the world, Bitcoin, has drawn a lot of interest as a potential investment. It has drawn individuals and institutions looking for diversification and expansion prospects due to its distinctive qualities, which include a restricted supply, decentralization, and the possibility for significant returns. The objective of this section is to examine the pros and cons of Bitcoin as an investment, outlining its benefits as well as its drawbacks.

Blockchain, a decentralized network that underpins Bitcoin, safely and openly records every transaction. Bitcoin is a digital asset that may be purchased, owned, and possibly sold for a profit as an investment. It is a unique investment choice because to its scarcity, divisible nature, and fungibility.

The price history of Bitcoin has been characterized by periods of noteworthy price volatility and price increase. Bitcoin has seen both quick growth and dramatic losses since its introduction, making it an appealing but risky investment. For assessing Bitcoin's potential as an investment asset, it is essential to comprehend its historical performance.

The possibility for significant returns is one of the main reasons people invest in Bitcoin. Due to its volatile nature, Bitcoin's price has increased significantly over time, providing the potential for big rewards for both early adopters and long-term holders.

Due to Bitcoin's low connection with conventional asset classes like stocks and bonds, diversification is possible. When traditional markets are failing, including Bitcoin in an investment portfolio might help lower total portfolio risk and possibly boost returns.

Due to Bitcoin's decentralized structure, investors can simply access the market. Investment in Bitcoin is open to everyone with an internet connection and a digital wallet. Also, Bitcoin works all over the world, giving investors access to a large, liquid market that is open 24/7.

Bitcoin is a desirable hedge against inflation and economic volatility due to its limited quantity and decentralized structure. Some investors look to Bitcoin as a store of value that might hold its purchasing power over time when governments and central banks undertake expansionary monetary policies.

For investors, the volatility of Bitcoin is a major concern. Price swings can be significant and quick, which might result in losses for individuals who are unprepared or don't manage risk well. High volatility may potentially deter institutional investment and widespread adoption.

The regulatory environment in which Bitcoin functions is still developing. Investors may be at risk due to uncertainty surrounding governmental rules, taxes, and legal frameworks. The value and applicability of Bitcoin as an investment asset may be impacted by changes in regulations or unfavorable governmental actions.

The market's demand is what ultimately determines the value of bitcoin. Bitcoin lacks intrinsic value derived from underlying assets or cash flows, in contrast to conventional investments like stocks or real estate. Because of how significantly market emotion and acceptance influence its value, it is prone to speculative bubbles and unexpected price changes.

The security of Bitcoin investments is at danger. Since Bitcoin is stored digitally, there is always a possibility that it will be stolen, hacked, or used in a scam. Investors should put a high priority on effective security measures, including utilizing reliable wallets, using two-factor authentication, and being on the lookout for phishing scams and other fraudulent schemes.

Investors thinking about Bitcoin should do some research and exercise caution. Becoming familiar with Bitcoin's technology, market dynamics, and potential risks is essential before investing money in this asset class. Making wise investing selections requires keeping up with market trends, legislative changes, and industry news.

Investors should carefully consider their risk tolerance and only devote a fraction of their portfolio to Bitcoin because of its volatility.

Investment in a single asset, such as Bitcoin, carries certain risks that can be reduced by diversification across various asset classes.

Having a long-term outlook is necessary when investing in bitcoin. The potential long-term advantages of keeping Bitcoin as an investment asset should not be overshadowed by short-term price volatility and market sentiment. Investing with patience and discipline can help you through this market's volatility.

Excitement and skepticism have both been generated by the development of Bitcoin as a form of investment. Bitcoin is an appealing investment due to its potential for high returns, benefits of diversity, accessibility, and inflation hedging. But given its volatility, regulatory issues, lack of intrinsic value, and security concerns, it is important to exercise caution while making decisions and managing risks. When considering Bitcoin as a component of their investing strategy, investors must assess the benefits and drawbacks, do extensive research, and apply caution, just like with any other investment.

Trading Bitcoin: Spot trading, futures, options

The pioneering cryptocurrency, Bitcoin, has become a very popular trading asset. Its extreme volatility, liquidity, and possibility for significant returns draw traders from all over the world. The objective of this section is to examine the various Bitcoin trading strategies, with a particular emphasis on spot trading, futures contracts, and options contracts. Understanding these trading instruments allows traders to navigate the Bitcoin market and take decisions that are based on their trading objectives.

Trading in Bitcoin entails purchasing and selling the digital currency with the intention of profiting from price fluctuations. The goal of traders is to forecast the movement of Bitcoin's price and place trades in that direction. Since Bitcoin trading is available 24/7, unlike traditional financial markets, traders can profit from price changes whenever they occur.

A variety of market participants, including retail traders, institutional investors, hedge funds, and algorithmic trading companies, are involved in the Bitcoin market. The market's accessibility and liquidity draw a wide variety of traders, which helps to create a thriving trading ecosystem.

Buying or selling Bitcoin for immediate delivery is referred to as spot trading, and settlement takes place "on the spot." In spot trading, participants acquire ownership of the digital asset by buying or selling actual Bitcoin. The simplest and most frequent method of trading Bitcoin is through spot markets, which include exchanging Bitcoin for fiat money or other cryptocurrencies.

The majority of spot trading takes place on bitcoin exchanges. These platforms offer a market area where vendors and purchasers can submit orders and complete transactions. Spot exchanges that are well-known include Coinbase, Binance, Kraken, and Bitstamp. To meet the demands of various traders, spot exchanges provide a variety of features, such as order types, trading pairs, and liquidity levels.

Trading methods like day trading, swing trading, and long-term holding are all possible with spot trading. To find probable entry and exit positions, traders might make use of technical analysis tools including price charts, indicators, and trend lines. Spot trading strategies can also be influenced by fundamental research, which entails evaluating news, market sentiment, and regulatory changes.

Futures contracts for Bitcoins are derivative products that let traders make bets on the price of the digital currency in the future. Futures contracts are a commitment to purchase or sell Bitcoin at a specific price and time in the future. Trading Bitcoin futures enables investors to profit from both rising and falling Bitcoin values by taking long (buy) and short (sell) positions.

On specialized futures platforms like the Chicago Mercantile Exchange (CME) and the Intercontinental Exchange (ICE), trading in bitcoin futures is done. The trading of Bitcoin futures contracts can be done in a controlled atmosphere on these exchanges. To access these markets, traders must first create an account with a futures broker.

The availability of leverage, which enables traders to hold a larger position with a smaller amount of funds, is one of the primary characteristics of Bitcoin futures trading. Leverage increases the likelihood of both gains and losses. Trading in Bitcoin futures frequently uses margin trading, which is borrowing money to open futures positions. However, because of the elevated risk involved with leverage and margin trading, traders must proceed with caution.

Futures contracts on Bitcoin can be used to manage risk. Hedgers can utilize futures contracts to hedge against price volatility, protecting their operations from unfavorable price changes, such Bitcoin miners or companies that accept Bitcoin payments.

Bitcoin option contracts give investors the option, but not the obligation, to purchase or sell Bitcoin at a predetermined price (strike price) within a predetermined time frame (expiration date). Options allow traders to be flexible in their trading strategies by letting them predict price changes or defend current positions.

Trading in bitcoin options occurs on specialized options exchanges like Deribit and LedgerX. These platforms give traders access to a market where they may purchase and sell options contracts. Similar to futures trading, opening an account with an options broker is required for traders to access these markets.

Buying call options (betting on price increase), buying put options (betting on price decrease), and selling options (generating income from premium collection) are just a few of the strategies that traders can use when trading Bitcoin options. When employing options methods, traders must carefully take into account their risk tolerance, time horizon, and market forecast.

The high volatility of Bitcoin presents both opportunities and risks for investors. Rapid price changes might bring about substantial gains or losses. The risks involved in trading in a volatile market must be managed and minimized by traders.

Regulation compliance could be necessary when trading Bitcoin futures and options. To avoid legal problems, traders should make sure they are aware of and following all applicable legislation in their area.

To protect their funds and reduce potential losses, traders should create solid risk management plans. Effective risk management requires accurate risk assessment, position sizing, and the implementation of stop-loss orders. Successful trading also requires ongoing education and keeping up with market developments.

Diverse opportunities exist in Bitcoin trading for traders to profit from price changes in the cryptocurrency market. Direct ownership of Bitcoin can be obtained through spot trading on cryptocurrency exchanges, but futures and options trading provide derivative instruments for speculating and risk management. Before starting a Bitcoin trading strategy, traders should carefully analyze their trading goals, risk tolerance, and market expertise. Each trading strategy has its own benefits and considerations. Traders can navigate the Bitcoin market more confidently and make wise trading decisions by being aware of the mechanics of spot trading, futures contracts, and options contracts.

Strategies for investing in Bitcoin: HODL, trading, dollar-cost averaging

The most popular cryptocurrency in the world, Bitcoin, has grown to be a desirable investment option for those looking to diversify their portfolios and profit from its future growth. However, carefully weighing various approaches is necessary before investing in Bitcoin. This section examines three well-liked methods of purchasing Bitcoin: trading, dollar-cost averaging, and HODLing (long-term holding). Investors can make well-informed choices that are in line with their investing objectives and risk tolerance by knowing these techniques.

The HODL approach is based on the notion of holding Bitcoin for an extended period of time with the expectation that its value would rise over time. HODLers put off the urge to sell during brief market fluctuations in favor of concentrating on the long-term potential of Bitcoin.

HODLing is motivated by the conviction that Bitcoin's supply is finite and that its price will rise in the future. The goal of HODLers is to capitalize on potential sizable long-term returns by holding onto Bitcoin for a long time. The idea that Bitcoin will continue to appreciate in value over time is the foundation of this strategy.

HODLing does come with certain risks, though. Because of the volatility of Bitcoin, there is a risk of losses for HODLers who do not carefully manage their assets during significant price swings. Successful HODLing requires emotional control, long-term thinking, and the capacity to withstand market downturns.

Trading in Bitcoin includes aggressively purchasing and selling the digital currency in order to benefit from swift price changes. To determine probable entry and exit opportunities for their transactions, traders examine market trends, technical indicators, and other elements.

Trading strategies come in a variety of forms, such as scalping, swing trading, and day trading. Day traders place numerous deals in a single day to take advantage of slight price fluctuations. Swing traders try to profit from medium-term price swings by holding positions for a few days to many weeks. Scalpers make money from slight price differences by making many fast deals.

Trading Bitcoin involves proficiency with technical analysis, tight risk management, and ongoing market monitoring. Risk must be carefully managed, trading techniques must be developed, and traders must be ready to accept possible losses. Successful trading requires emotional control, lifelong learning, and market-conditions adaptation.

Regardless of the price of Bitcoin, an investor uses the Dollar-Cost Averaging (DCA) investment technique to consistently buy a set quantity of the cryptocurrency over time. Investors can buy more Bitcoin when prices are low and less when prices are high by regularly investing a fixed amount.

With DCA, there is no longer a need to time the market and less risk associated with making sizable investments at unfavorable prices. By allowing them to average their purchase price over time, investors can potentially lessen the effects of short-term market volatility. Using a disciplined strategy like DCA, investors can take part in Bitcoin's long-term growth.

The size of the investment, the frequency of purchases, and the length of the investment period are all things that DCA takes into account. In certain forms of DCA, the investment amount is increased during market downturns, or the approach is changed in response to market conditions.

When deciding on a Bitcoin investing strategy, investors should consider their time horizon, investment goals, and risk tolerance. HODLing is appropriate for long-term investors who can handle market volatility, whereas trading calls for active participation and risk management abilities. For investors looking for long-term exposure to Bitcoin, DCA is a more passive technique.

Specific risk management procedures should be put into place for the selected strategy. This entails establishing sensible investment objectives, diversifying investment holdings, and using stop-loss orders while trading. Effective risk management requires regular portfolio reviews, continued education, and staying current on market developments.

The legal and regulatory implications of investing in Bitcoin, such as taxation, reporting requirements, and compliance with local rules, must also be taken into account by investors. In order to assure compliance and prevent legal problems, it is essential to understand the legal system in one's jurisdiction.

Investing in Bitcoin presents possibilities for development and diversity. HODLing, trading, and dollar-cost averaging are three different techniques that can be used depending on the risk tolerance and preferences of the investor. In contrast to trading, which seeks to profit from short-term price fluctuations, DCA offers a disciplined approach for gradually accumulating Bitcoin. Every technique has unique benefits, difficulties, and risk-management considerations. Investors may navigate the Bitcoin market and make wise investment selections by carefully analyzing these strategies and matching them with their investing goals.

CHAPTER VII
Risk Management in Bitcoin Investment

Understanding volatility and market risks

Due to its potential for high returns, Bitcoin, the first cryptocurrency, has attracted a lot of attention as an investment instrument. Investors must, however, properly comprehend and assess the market risks and volatility of Bitcoin. The goal of this section is to give readers a thorough grasp of market risk and volatility when investing in Bitcoin. Investors can make informed judgments and successfully manage the risks related to investing in Bitcoin by being aware of these issues.

Rapid and large price changes on the cryptocurrency market define Bitcoin's volatility. Bitcoin's volatility is influenced by a number of variables, including as market demand and sentiment, legislative changes, macroeconomic considerations, technological improvements, media attention, and the overall sentiment of market participants. It is essential to comprehend the volatility of Bitcoin historically in order to evaluate the potential risks and benefits of investing in the cryptocurrency.

Since its launch, Bitcoin's price has fluctuated noticeably. Historical data shows times of abrupt price corrections after quick price increases. For investors, these price changes present both possibilities and risks. Therefore, for effective Bitcoin investment, knowing and controlling volatility are crucial.

Investors should be aware of the numerous market risks associated with investing in Bitcoin. The market liquidity and price impact, security concerns, technology risks, market manipulation and fraud are among these hazards. They also include regulatory and legal risks.

The regulatory landscape surrounding Bitcoin is changing, which poses risks in the regulatory and legal sectors. Regulation changes or government interference may have an effect on the price and use of Bitcoin. To ensure compliance and avoid potential legal problems, investors need to be updated on the legal and regulatory requirements in their respective jurisdictions.

Investment in Bitcoin is difficult because of market liquidity and price impact. The market may become illiquid during times of extreme volatility, which can cause price swings to be exaggerated and make it harder to execute trades at desired prices. Large buy or sell orders can significantly affect the price of Bitcoin, increasing slippage and potentially causing losses for investors.

Buying Bitcoin carries inherent security risks. Cryptocurrencies are prone to hacking attempts, thefts, and scams because of their decentralized structure. Investors should put a high priority on effective security measures, including utilizing reliable wallets, using two-factor authentication, and being on the lookout for phishing scams and other fraudulent schemes.

Blockchain, the technology that underpins Bitcoin, carries certain technological hazards. The reliability and efficiency of the Bitcoin network can be impacted by software defects, network congestion, and scaling issues. To reduce associated risks, investors should be informed about advancements in technology, potential risks, and upgrades.

Market risks unique to the cryptocurrency market include fraud and market manipulation. Due to its decentralized structure and low level of regulation, Bitcoin is susceptible to fraud and market manipulation. To avoid fraudulent schemes, investors must perform due diligence, undertake in-depth research, and interact with trusted platforms.

Investors can employ a variety of risk management measures to manage the volatility and market hazards associated with Bitcoin investments.

A well-known risk management technique is diversification. Investors can lessen the potential influence of Bitcoin's volatility on their overall investment performance by distributing their assets across other asset classes. Investments in more established assets like equities, bonds, and real estate can help reduce the risks brought on by the volatility of the Bitcoin market.

Risk management is critically dependent on asset allocation and risk tolerance. Investors should carefully consider their risk tolerance and investment objectives when allocating funds to Bitcoin. Setting suitable asset allocation goals in accordance with one's level of risk tolerance might aid in balancing the possible benefits and risks of investing in Bitcoins throughout one's whole portfolio.

Before making a Bitcoin investment, risk analysis and due research are crucial. Investors should do extensive study, weigh the risks and rewards, and keep up with market trends, legislative changes, and advancements in technology. Investors can make wise decisions and efficiently manage their investments by evaluating the potential risks.

In volatile markets, prospective losses can be restricted by risk mitigation methods like stop-loss orders. A stop-loss order is a directive to automatically sell Bitcoin if its price drops below a particular threshold. During market downturns, this technique aids in preventing investors from suffering severe losses.

Continuous education and awareness are essential for managing market risks and volatility effectively when investing in bitcoin.

To stay informed about the shifting market dynamics for Bitcoin, investors should pursue continuous learning. Understanding technical analysis, market trends, fundamental analysis, and risk management techniques fall under this category. Investors can reduce risks, adapt to changing market conditions, and make informed decisions with the aid of education.

Assessing potential risks and possibilities in the Bitcoin business requires being current on market news, industry trends, legislative developments, and technology advancements. To keep informed, investors should subscribe to reliable news outlets, participate in pertinent forums, and interact with the larger cryptocurrency community.

Investors considering a Bitcoin investment must have a thorough understanding of market risk and volatility. Investors must carefully weigh the risks and advantages of this asset class in order to understand why Bitcoin is so volatile. Market risks, such as those related to regulations and the law, liquidity, security, technology, and market manipulation, necessitate careful risk management.

Diversification, asset allocation, risk assessment, and the use of risk-mitigation tools are a few examples of risk management techniques that investors might employ. Successful risk management depends on lifelong learning and keeping up with the Bitcoin market. Investors can navigate the volatile Bitcoin market and successfully manage the risks related to their investments by taking a cautious and knowledgeable approach.

Risk management strategies: Diversification, stop losses, etc.

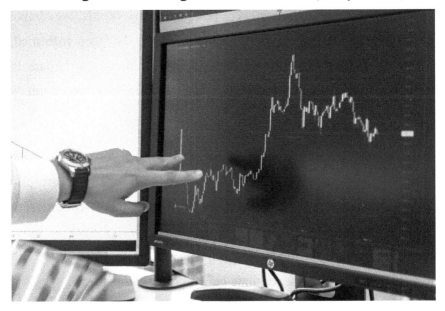

A thorough understanding of risk management techniques is necessary for investing in the financial markets, especially the volatile Bitcoin market. The major risk management techniques discussed in this section are diversification, stop losses, position sizing, hedging, and thorough due diligence. Investors can successfully reduce possible losses and increase their overall success in the Bitcoin market by putting these strategies into practice.

Allocating investments among a variety of asset classes is a fundamental risk management method called diversification. Investors can spread their risk over a variety of assets and limit their exposure to any one investment, such as Bitcoin, by diversifying their portfolios. This approach lessens the potential effects of a single investment's poor performance on the portfolio as a whole and helps guard against market volatility. Investors can build a more well-rounded and durable investment portfolio by diversifying.

With the use of stop losses, investors can set up fixed exit points for their investments, which is a crucial risk management tool. With a stop loss order, the broker is told to sell an asset if the price drops below a particular level. Investors can reduce their potential losses and protect their funds in the event of unfavorable price changes by establishing stop losses. Stop losses ensure that investors exit their positions when required to reduce losses, helping to enforce discipline and eliminate emotional decision-making.

Position sizing is the process of allocating money to specific investments. Investors can choose the right size of their stakes in numerous assets, including Bitcoin, by carefully evaluating their tolerance for risk and investing goals. An investor is not exposed to an excessive amount of risk through any one investment, due to proper position sizing. Investors can maintain a balanced portfolio and lessen the potential impact of any one investment on their overall wealth by minimizing their risk exposure through position sizing.

A risk management technique called "hedging" is holding positions to counteract prospective losses in other investments. Investors can hedge their positions in the Bitcoin market by employing a number of strategies. For instance, they might employ options or futures contracts to protect themselves against prospective price drops. Investors can lower their exposure to downside risk while still preserving the desired amount of participation in the possible upside of their assets by using hedging strategies. Hedging serves as a sort of insurance, defending investors from unfavorable changes in the market.

Any investment endeavor must implement thorough due diligence as a key risk management strategy, and buying Bitcoin is no different. Before choosing an investment, investors should do extensive study and analysis. This entails analyzing Bitcoin's fundamentals, comprehending the underlying technology, figuring out market movements, and keeping up with legislative changes. Effective due diligence aids investors in selecting assets, identifying potential hazards, and avoiding risky or dishonest ones.

A key component of risk management is assessing the risk-reward ratio. Before investing money, investors must carefully weigh the risks and rewards that could result. Risks are frequently higher for investments with higher potential returns. Investors must establish a balance between prospective gains and the amount of risk they are willing to take. Investors can make decisions that are in line with their investing objectives and risk tolerance by completing a thorough risk-reward analysis.

Continuous monitoring and periodic portfolio reviews are necessary for the continuing process of risk management. Investors should periodically review the performance of their holdings, analyze the state of the market, and alter their portfolios as needed. Investors can spot potential risks, capture opportunities, and adjust their risk management methods to changing market conditions by keeping a close eye on their investments. The investing strategy is kept in line with the investor's goals and risk tolerance through routine portfolio evaluations.

For successful investing in the cryptocurrency market, including Bitcoin, proper risk management measures must be put into practice. Important risk management methods include diversification, stop losses, position sizing, hedging, thorough due diligence, risk-reward analysis, and continual monitoring. Investors can reduce possible losses, protect their funds, and increase their prospects of long-term success in the cryptocurrency market by combining these strategies and customizing them to individual risk profiles and investing objectives. Investors can deal with the volatility nature of Bitcoin investment with greater confidence and accomplish their financial goals if they have a thorough risk management strategy in place.

Regulatory risks: Global overview

The regulatory landscape in which the cryptocurrency industry, including Bitcoin, functions is complex and differs between countries. Investors must be aware of the regulatory risks related to Bitcoin as governments and regulatory agencies struggle to deal with the emergence of cryptocurrencies. This section offers a thorough analysis of worldwide regulatory issues in the cryptocurrency industry, looking at the various stances adopted by various nations and their potential effects on Bitcoin investors.

The diverse approaches and levels of acceptability across nations define the regulatory landscape for cryptocurrencies.

Multiple agencies in developed nations like the United States are in charge of regulatory oversight. Securities offerings, derivatives trading, and taxation relating to cryptocurrencies are heavily regulated by the Securities and Exchange Commission (SEC), the Commodity Futures Trading Commission (CFTC), and the Internal Revenue Service (IRS).

The Fifth Anti-Money Laundering Directive (AMLD5) has been put into effect in the European Union (EU) to include cryptocurrencies in the scope of anti-money laundering laws. EU members are also creating their own rules and licensing standards for cryptocurrency exchanges and service providers.

Initial coin offerings (ICOs), cryptocurrency exchanges, and mining activities have all been outlawed in developing nations like China where the government has taken a strong position against cryptocurrencies. However, there is also a growing desire to investigate how blockchain technology might be used in different industries.

India has adopted a cautious stance; the Reserve Bank of India (RBI) initially forbade banks from doing business with entities associated to cryptocurrencies. The ban was ultimately lifted by the Indian Supreme Court, allowing both private persons and commercial entities to trade cryptocurrencies.

Investors in Bitcoin are subject to a number of regulatory concerns that could have an impact on both their investments and the wider cryptocurrency market.

Uncertainty generated by Bitcoin's changing regulatory environment causes market volatility. The price of Bitcoin and the general sentiment of the market can be strongly impacted by regulatory actions, announcements, or changes in the legislation. To anticipate potential risks and market reactions, investors must stay up to date on regulatory developments.

Compliance and reporting requirements are frequently placed on Bitcoin firms and exchanges by regulatory frameworks. Know Your Customer (KYC) procedures, anti-money laundering (AML) controls, and transaction reporting are a few examples of these regulations. The expenses and administrative hurdles related to compliance may have an effect on how bitcoin businesses run and may indirectly harm investors.

Regulations that impose trade and exchange prohibitions or trading limitations on cryptocurrencies have the potential to reduce the accessibility and liquidity of the Bitcoin markets. Investors in countries with strict regulations may encounter difficulties when purchasing, selling, or holding Bitcoin, which may limit their ability to take advantage of market opportunities.

Different jurisdictions have different cryptocurrency tax laws. The tax implications of investing in Bitcoin, including capital gains taxes, reporting requirements, and prospective tax audits, must be understood by investors. Penalties and legal issues may result from failure to abide by tax requirements.

Investors in Bitcoin have numerous options for navigating regulatory risks.

Following reliable news outlets, trade journals, and official regulatory body announcements will help Bitcoin investors stay up to date on regulatory changes. Investors can foresee potential dangers and modify their investing strategy as necessary by being aware of regulatory developments.

Prior to investing in Bitcoin, thorough due diligence is essential. Investors should select trustworthy cryptocurrency exchanges, be aware of their jurisdiction's regulatory laws, and follow KYC and AML protocols. Investors can reduce their risk of legal issues and protect their money by complying with regulatory standards.

Diversification continues to be an important risk management strategy. Investors in Bitcoin should think about diversifying their holdings across several cryptocurrencies, conventional assets, and geographical areas. Investors can lessen the effect of regulatory risks on their overall investment performance by diversifying their holdings.

Participating in advocacy efforts can assist in creating beneficial regulatory frameworks. Investors in Bitcoin can join professional organizations, take part in policymaker debates, and express their concerns and recommendations. Investors may be able to influence rules in a way that fosters innovation while preserving investor protection by actively participating in the regulatory discussion.

The cryptocurrency sector is filled with regulatory risks, and buyers of Bitcoin must go through a complex legal environment. Different nations' strategies differ greatly from one another, posing problems and uncertainty. For regulatory risks to be reduced, it is essential to have a thorough understanding of their possible effects, keep informed, do due diligence, ensure compliance, diversify investments, and take part in advocacy activities. Investors may position themselves to handle the changing regulatory climate and take advantage of Bitcoin's long-term potential by actively minimizing regulatory risks.

CHAPTER VIII
Bitcoin Forks and Alternatives

What is a Bitcoin fork? Explanation with examples: Bitcoin Cash, Bitcoin SV

Over the course of its existence, the first cryptocurrency, Bitcoin, has undergone a number of forks. The foundations of these forks, such Bitcoin Cash (BCH) and Bitcoin SV (BSV), came from the original Bitcoin network and resulted in the creation of distinct cryptocurrencies. In order to provide readers a thorough knowledge of Bitcoin forks, this section will discuss their nature, the causes of them, and the specific cases of Bitcoin Cash and Bitcoin SV.

When the original Bitcoin blockchain is split into two different chains, a fork occurs, leading to the formation of a new cryptocurrency in addition to the original Bitcoin. This happens as a result of a divergence in the blockchain's transaction history caused by a change in the protocol rules governing the Bitcoin network.

Forks in the Bitcoin network can be either soft or hard. A soft fork is an upgrade that is backward-compatible and adds new rules while still working with the current blockchain. A hard fork, on the other hand, is an upgrade that is not backward-compatible and necessitates that all users embrace the new guidelines. This causes the blockchain to permanently diverge.

The continuous scaling controversy is one of the main causes of Bitcoin forks. Conversations over the network's scalability have been prompted by Bitcoin's constrained block size and transaction throughput. Divergent methods to solving this problem as a result of varying viewpoints have given rise to forks that try to produce cryptocurrencies with improved scalability.

Disagreements over the original Bitcoin network's governance or protocol updates can potentially lead to forks in the cryptocurrency. Different perspectives on the protocol's block sizes, transaction costs, consensus techniques, and other elements may result in the development of distinct cryptocurrencies with different set of regulations.

The original Bitcoin network underwent a hard fork in August 2017, leading to the creation of Bitcoin Cash (BCH). By boosting the block size from 1MB to 8MB, it was able to increase transaction throughput while also addressing Bitcoin's scalability issues.

Due to its higher block size, which allows for more transactions to be completed each block, Bitcoin Cash sets itself apart from Bitcoin. Compared to the original Bitcoin, this higher block size is intended to offer transactions that are quicker and less expensive. A separate difficulty adjustment method is also used by Bitcoin Cash, making it more responsive to changes in network hash rate.

A committed community of developers, miners, and users have supported Bitcoin Cash. It is now widely accepted as a form of payment and has been incorporated into a number of exchanges for cryptocurrencies. Regarding its scalability solutions and centralization issues, it has however also generated debates and criticisms.

In November 2018, the Bitcoin Cash blockchain underwent a contentious hard fork, leading to the creation of Bitcoin SV (BSV), or Bitcoin Satoshi Vision. The main goal of Bitcoin SV was to restore what its supporters believed was Satoshi Nakamoto's original vision for the Bitcoin.

With an emphasis on bigger block sizes and the scaling possibilities of on-chain transactions, Bitcoin SV seeks to maintain the original Bitcoin system. It aims to make it possible for businesses and applications to be created on top of the Bitcoin blockchain while strictly sticking to minimal protocol changes.

A particular group of developers and companies that support Bitcoin SV do so because they believe it has the potential to scale and is consistent with the original Bitcoin concept. However, it has also been the subject of disagreements and critiques, including arguments about its management and reservations about its centralization.

The market for cryptocurrencies has changed as a result of Bitcoin forks like Bitcoin Cash and Bitcoin SV emerging. These forks have given rise to other cryptocurrencies with specialized goals and a range of user preferences. Additionally, they have given traders and investors chances to diversify their holdings and take part in the growth of other blockchain ecosystems.

Disagreements and conflicts within the cryptocurrency community have been caused by Bitcoin forks. Supporters of various forks frequently have divergent opinions on the scalability, governance, and course of the Bitcoin project. These differences have sparked continuing conversations and disagreements within the community, which have influenced how the cryptocurrency ecosystem will develop in the future.

Forks of the Bitcoin network like Bitcoin Cash and Bitcoin SV are important developments in the evolution of the cryptocurrency market. They developed from various perspectives and methods for dealing with protocol updates, governance, and scalability. Forks bring complications and divides among the cryptocurrency ecosystem while also opening doors for innovation and customization. Investors and enthusiasts can navigate the changing cryptocurrency landscape and make wise choices about their participation in these various blockchain ecosystems by comprehending the nature, motivations, and examples of Bitcoin forks.

Overview of major cryptocurrencies other than Bitcoin

While Bitcoin continues to be the most popular and significant cryptocurrency, there are many more digital assets with distinctive features and applications available on the larger cryptocurrency market. This section explores the history, distinctive characteristics, and possible uses of the most significant cryptocurrencies besides Bitcoin. Investors may explore alternate investing opportunities in the changing world of digital assets by comprehending the variety of cryptocurrencies.

The decentralized platform Ethereum (ETH), introduced in 2015 by Vitalik Buterin, facilitates the creation of smart contracts and decentralized applications (DApps). The idea of programmable blockchain was proposed, enabling programmers to build and launch their applications on the Ethereum network.

The unique feature of Ethereum is its capacity to carry out Turing-complete smart contracts, facilitating the creation of decentralized applications in numerous sectors. Additionally, the ERC-20 standard was developed, simplifying the development of new coins and enabling crowdfunding through initial coin offerings (ICOs). Scalability improvements for Ethereum and network updates like Ethereum 2.0 are intended to improve transaction throughput and alleviate network constraints.

Decentralized governance, non-fungible tokens (NFTs), supply chain management, and decentralized finance (DeFi) are just some of the applications where Ethereum has found use. Its programmability and flexibility make it a well-liked platform for entrepreneurs and developers looking to create tokenized ecosystems and decentralized applications.

Launched in 2012, Ripple (XRP) is a cryptocurrency as well as a digital payment protocol. Its main goal is to make international money transfers and remittances quick and affordable. The XRP Ledger, which offers real-time gross settlement and currency exchange capabilities, is the distributed ledger platform on which Ripple runs.

By providing quick transaction settlements and affordable fees, Ripple distinguishes itself and attracts cross-border business. Faster transaction confirmation times are made possible by the Ripple Protocol Consensus Algorithm (RPCA), which is its consensus algorithm. With a focus on collaborations with financial institutions, Ripple seeks to connect conventional financial systems with blockchain technology.

Banks and other financial institutions have started using ripple's technology to streamline remittances and international money transfers. By lowering settlement times and transaction costs, it seeks to increase the effectiveness of conventional financial systems. The network of Ripple also has the ability to tokenize assets and increase liquidity between multiple currencies.

Charlie Lee invented Litecoin (LTC) in 2011, and it is frequently referred to as the "silver to Bitcoin's gold." It is a peer-to-peer cryptocurrency that resembles Bitcoin in many ways, including its use of blockchain technology and open-source design. But Litecoin sets itself apart with a few technical characteristics.

Litecoin uses the Scrypt hashing algorithm and has faster block generation times, making it more resistant to specialized mining hardware. Compared to Bitcoin, these attributes lead to faster transaction confirmations and a bigger total coin supply. Prior to being incorporated into Bitcoin, new features will first be tested out on Litecoin.

Litecoin is primarily utilized as a store of value and as a medium of commerce. It is suited for everyday transactions due to its quicker transaction times, and investors looking for a digital asset with a track record will find it interesting due to its resemblance to Bitcoin.

A blockchain platform called Cardano (ADA), which was introduced in 2017, seeks to offer a safe and reliable platform for the creation of decentralized applications and smart contracts. Charles Hoskinson, a founding member of Ethereum, founded it.

Cardano distinguishes itself from other blockchains through its emphasis on scientific research, peer-reviewed development, and layered architecture that increases security and scalability. It uses the Ouroboros proof-of-stake consensus mechanism, which aims to be both safe and energy-efficient. The development timeline for Cardano has several phases, with a focus on sustainability and governance.

The goal of Cardano is to make it easier to create decentralized applications and to provide infrastructure for fields like supply chain management, identity verification, and governance systems. It serves as a platform for creating reliable and scalable blockchain solutions because of its concentration on academic research and strict development procedures.

The cryptocurrency exchange Binance introduced Binance Coin (BNB) in 2017, and it runs on the Binance Chain and acts as the ecosystem's native utility token. Binance Coin was initially released as an ERC-20 token on the Ethereum blockchain before moving to its own platform.

Reduced trading fees, participation in token sales, and access to advanced features on the Binance exchange are just a few of the perks that Binance Coin makes available within the Binance ecosystem. On the Binance Chain, it has also been used to create tokenized assets.

Within the Binance ecosystem, Binance Coin primarily functions as a utility token that rewards and incentivizes users of the Binance exchange. Due to its affiliation with one of the biggest cryptocurrency exchanges, it has grown in popularity and is used to access a variety of services and goods on the Binance platform.

Other significant cryptocurrencies still have value and potential despite Bitcoin's dominance in the cryptocurrency market. In addition to others, Ethereum, Ripple, Litecoin, Cardano, and Binance Coin each have unique features and applications that address specific aspects of the digital economy. Investors have the chance to diversify their portfolios within the changing cryptocurrency landscape by having a better understanding of these significant cryptocurrencies beyond Bitcoin. These alternative digital assets provide special investing opportunities as the cryptocurrency market expands and have the potential to have disruptive uses in many areas of the global economy.

Altcoins vs Bitcoin: Differences and similarities

Since the introduction of cryptocurrencies, Bitcoin has dominated the market for digital assets. However, the rise of alternative cryptocurrencies, also referred to as altcoins, has given the cryptocurrency market a new dimension. In order to shed light on their distinctive characteristics, use cases, and the overall relationship between these digital assets, this section examines the differences as well as similarities between altcoins and Bitcoin.

A decentralized digital currency intended to function as a means of exchange, Bitcoin was developed in 2009 by an unidentified individual or group of individuals known only as Satoshi Nakamoto. With no need for intermediaries, it intends to offer a peer-to-peer electronic payment system that enables safe and borderless transactions.

All cryptocurrencies other than Bitcoin are referred to as "altcoins," a term derived from "alternative coins." These digital assets were developed to overcome particular constraints or explore different use cases outside of those provided by Bitcoin.

Compared to Bitcoin, altcoins frequently provide new technology and advancements. They might make use of various hashing techniques, consensus processes, or scalability solutions. For instance, while Ripple concentrated on enabling quick cross-border transactions, Ethereum added smart contracts.

With the highest market capitalization, Bitcoin continues to rule the cryptocurrency industry. When taken as a whole, altcoins make up a lesser portion of the market capitalization. However, several alternative coins, like Ethereum and Ripple, have attained significant prices and market acceptance.

The main purposes of Bitcoin are to act as a store of value and a decentralized digital currency. On the other hand, alternative coins frequently focus on particular sectors or uses. For instance, Litecoin places an emphasis on quicker transaction confirmations, but altcoins like Monero that prioritize privacy seek to increase anonymity.

Altcoins are created on top of the same decentralized blockchain networks as Bitcoin. They operate decentralized and without middlemen, guaranteeing the immutability, security, and transparency of all transactions. The cryptocurrency ecosystem is built around this common trait.

Due to elements like market sentiment, governmental changes, and technological improvements, Bitcoin and other cryptocurrencies are prone to significant levels of volatility. In an effort to benefit from price changes, investors frequently participate in speculative trading.

Within the cryptocurrency market, trading and investing options are offered by Bitcoin and other cryptocurrencies. Utilizing the potential growth of these digital assets, investors can diversify their portfolios by incorporating a mix of Bitcoin and alternative cryptocurrencies.

Due to its dominance in the cryptocurrency market, Bitcoin has become the standard and point of comparison for the performance and pricing of altcoins. The price of Bitcoin frequently affects the general market sentiment, which affects the pricing of altcoins.

The innovation and expansion of the larger cryptocurrency ecosystem is facilitated by altcoins. They study various use cases, propose fresh technology, and extend the capabilities of blockchain applications. Successful altcoins could inspire additional development in the sector, maybe leading to modifications or additions to Bitcoin itself.

Significant price volatility affects both Bitcoin and alternative cryptocurrencies, which can be risky for investors. Due to the growing and developing nature of the cryptocurrency industry, there is a need for investors to properly manage their risk exposure.

In many jurisdictions, the regulatory environment surrounding cryptocurrencies, such as Bitcoin and altcoins, is still unclear. Risks and uncertainties may be introduced by regulatory measures or legal challenges that affect how these digital assets are viewed by the market and how they are used.

Altcoins have evolved to offer distinctive features, investigate other use cases, and promote innovation within the ecosystem, despite the fact that Bitcoin continues to retain a dominant position in the cryptocurrency industry. While altcoins add to the variety and growth of the cryptocurrency environment, Bitcoin serves as the standard. Investors can navigate the shifting market, diversify their holdings, and profit from the potential growth and revolutionary power of digital assets by being aware of the differences and similarities between Bitcoin and altcoins. The link between Bitcoin and altcoins will influence the future of decentralized finance and the wider use of blockchain technology as the cryptocurrency ecosystem develops.

CHAPTER
IX
Privacy, Security, and
Legal Aspects of Bitcoin

Privacy in Bitcoin transactions: How much is there really?

As a decentralized and open-source cryptocurrency, Bitcoin has frequently been linked to privacy issues. Although Bitcoin transactions are visible on a public blockchain, there is continuous discussion about the level of privacy they provide. This section analyzes the privacy features of Bitcoin transactions, considers their drawbacks, and covers the various methods employed to increase transaction privacy.

Anyone can access transaction data on the public blockchain for Bitcoin, including sender and recipient addresses, transaction amounts, and timestamps. The network's immutability and reliability are enhanced by this transparency.

Pseudonymous transactions on the Bitcoin network employ cryptographic addresses to identify users rather than their real names. The real-world identities hidden behind the addresses are typically not explicitly disclosed, even though transactions are publicly recorded.

Despite the anonymity of Bitcoin addresses, there are numerous ways to connect transactions. Address reuse, in which a user uses the same address for several different transactions, can help identify and trace those activities. Blockchain analysis methods can also be used to link addresses and examine transaction flows, potentially disclosing information about a user's activities and spending habits.

The public ledger can be analyzed using blockchain analysis tools to spot patterns, such as the movement of money, the location of centralized exchanges, and the monitoring of illegal activity. The confidentiality of Bitcoin transactions may be compromised by this study, which may also make private data public.

By mixing the coins of several users together, coin mixing or tumbling services aim to increase privacy by making it difficult to track individual transactions. By breaking the connection between input and output addresses, these services offer some level of anonymity. Users must have trust that the mixing service won't compromise their privacy despite the fact that their effectiveness can vary.

Stealth addresses are cryptographic methods for increasing transaction anonymity in Bitcoin. For every transaction, they generate a different address, making it difficult to connect the sender's and recipient's addresses.

It can be difficult to distinguish between different inputs and outputs when using CoinJoins since several users combine their transactions into a single transaction. By obscuring the connection between the sender and destination addresses, this method offers a certain level of privacy.

Confidential Transactions (CT) encrypt transaction amounts using cryptographic methods. By hiding the precise transaction values, CT gives Bitcoin transactions an additional layer of privacy. On the Bitcoin network, this strategy is not yet commonly used.

Network analysis can still find trends and link transactions despite privacy-enhancing methods, potentially compromising privacy. Modern blockchain analysis methods and tools are constantly developing, posing a threat to the effectiveness of current privacy protections.

Techniques for improving privacy frequently call either the use of outside services or extra technological layers. Users must put their trust in these organizations, which raises concerns about their security, dependability, and risk of information leaks or data breaches.

Regulations may be in contradiction with privacy safeguards used in Bitcoin transactions, especially in countries that have Know Your Customer (KYC) and Anti-Money Laundering (AML) laws. Exchanges and service providers might be obliged to follow these rules, which would reduce the amount of privacy choices offered to users.

Schnorr signatures will be added to Bitcoin, which is expected to improve security and scalability. Schnorr signatures combine numerous signature inputs into a single signature, enabling more effective coin mixing and enhancing anonymity.

Off-chain transactions that use Layer 2 technologies, like the Lightning Network, are quicker and more private. By allowing users to carry out several transactions without publishing each one to the public blockchain, these technologies improve user privacy.

It is essential for Bitcoin users to increase understanding of privacy threats and accessible privacy-enhancing measures. Users can be empowered to make thoughtful decisions and protect their privacy by being informed about best practices, privacy tools, and the restrictions of privacy measures.

The issue of privacy in Bitcoin transactions has many aspects. Bitcoin provides pseudonymity and transparency, but the degree of privacy is susceptible to a number of restrictions and difficulties. The privacy of Bitcoin transactions may be compromised by blockchain analysis tools and public blockchain analysis. However, these risks can be somewhat reduced by using privacy-enhancing strategies like coin mixing, stealth addresses, CoinJoins, and private transactions. Future innovations, like as Layer 2 solutions and Schnorr signatures, have the potential to further improve transaction privacy for Bitcoin. In order to protect privacy and provide Bitcoin users more power, users must be informed about privacy issues, best practices, and available tools. The difficulty of balancing privacy concerns with legal compliance has to be explored further. Addressing privacy concerns in Bitcoin transactions will be essential for promoting adoption, confidence, and the full potential of decentralized digital currencies as the cryptocurrency ecosystem continues to develop.

Best practices for security: Protecting wallets, avoiding scams

The importance of protecting digital wallet security and avoiding frauds has increased as interest in cryptocurrency rises. This section examines the best security methods in the cryptocurrency industry, concentrating on wallet security and avoiding scams. Users may protect their funds and confidently navigate the landscape of digital assets by adhering to these best practices.

Cryptocurrency wallets come in a variety of forms, such as software wallets (desktop and mobile), hardware wallets, and web wallets. Selecting the best type of wallet requires an understanding of its qualities and security features.

Important parts that provide access to cryptocurrency funds are private keys. To avoid illegal access, users must safely store and manage their private keys. Best practices for increased security include the usage of hardware wallets, strong passwords, and offline storage.

It's crucial to make secure, unique passwords for wallets. Long, complicated passwords with a mix of capital and lowercase letters, numbers, and special characters are recommended. Keeping personal information and frequent phrases to yourself offers an extra layer of security.

Wallets are more secure when Two-Factor Authentication (2FA) is enabled. Users are required to submit a second form of verification, such as a code given to their mobile device, in order to access their funds by connecting the wallet to a trusted device or application.

It's essential to keep wallet software updated if you want to safeguard against vulnerabilities and exploits. Users should make sure they are using the most recent version of the wallet because developers frequently release upgrades to fix security issues.

By storing private keys offline, offline storage (cold wallets), such as hardware wallets or paper wallets, improve security. Due to their lack of internet connectivity, these wallets are less vulnerable to malware and hacking efforts.

Phishing attacks use fraudulent websites, emails, or messages to trick users into revealing their private keys or other sensitive information. Users should exercise caution, confirm the legitimacy of websites, double-check email senders, and refrain from clicking any suspicious links.

Users should do some research before participating in any cryptocurrency initiative or investment offer. Potential scams can be spotted by confirming the validity of projects, evaluating the dependability of the team, and reviewing evaluations and ratings from the public.

When interacting with cryptocurrency exchanges and wallets, secure communication is essential. Avoiding public Wi-Fi networks, using encrypted communication methods, and being cautious when sharing sensitive information can all help prevent data breaches and eavesdropping.

Maintaining security requires ongoing education on the ever changing cryptocurrency landscape. Users are better prepared to make wise judgments if they stay informed about new scams, security concerns, and industry best practices.

Users can learn from experts, get advice, and stay up to date on potential concerns by taking part in cryptocurrency groups and forums. Assembling a supportive and cooperative community of like-minded people promotes a collaborative atmosphere for raising security awareness.

Wallets, gadgets, and online accounts should all undergo routine security audits to find any possible vulnerabilities. Users should check their access rights, update their security settings, and keep an eye out for any unusual activity.

Users are essential to protecting the larger cryptocurrency community. Sharing information about potential hazards and reporting scams, suspicious websites, or phishing attempts to the appropriate authorities can help spread awareness and stop others from becoming victims of scams.

A proactive and watchful strategy is necessary to safeguard cryptocurrency wallets and prevent scams. Users can greatly improve the security of their funds by putting best practices into effect, including as using strong passwords, enabling 2FA, routinely updating wallet software, and employing offline storage options. Keeping an eye out for phishing efforts, doing extensive research, and staying up to date on new risks all help create a safer environment for cryptocurrencies. To maintain a secure and reliable environment, education, community involvement, and frequent security assessments are crucial. Individuals can confidently navigate the cryptocurrency ecosystem, protect their funds, and contribute to the overall security of the community of digital assets by adhering to certain recommended practices.

Legal considerations: Bitcoin and tax, legality across the world

Understanding the legal concerns surrounding cryptocurrencies, particularly those related to taxation and legality, is essential as Bitcoin and other cryptocurrencies acquire wider acceptance. In this section, the legal environment surrounding Bitcoin is examined, along with the tax implications, legislative frameworks, and international legality of Bitcoin. People can ensure compliance and make educated decisions about their connection with Bitcoin by looking at these legal considerations.

Tax authorities from all across the world have debated how to categorize Bitcoin for taxation. The classification differs between jurisdictions; some perceive it as a form of currency, while others view it as a piece of property, a commodity, or a financial asset. The categorization has effects on how Bitcoin transactions are taxed.

All types of Bitcoin transactions, such as buying, selling, trading, mining, and accepting Bitcoin in exchange for goods or services, might result in various taxable events. Depending on the individual event and the country's tax regulations, there are various tax implications. When selling Bitcoin for fiat currency, for instance, capital gains tax may be due, and when using Bitcoin to pay for goods or services, value-added tax (VAT) may be charged.

The sale or exchange of Bitcoin may be subject to capital gains tax in a number of jurisdictions. Taxes are charged on profits generated when selling Bitcoin for more money than it cost to get it, although losses may be deducted. The holding duration and the taxpayer's income level are just two examples of variables that can affect the tax rate for capital gains.

Tax authorities often demand that people declare and include their Bitcoin transactions in their tax returns. Giving information on transaction amounts, dates, and any gains or losses is part of this. Inaccurate Bitcoin transaction reporting can have penalties and perhaps legal consequences.

The legal position of Bitcoin varies greatly amongst nations, with some accepting it, others taking a cautious stance, and some outright prohibiting or restricting its use. To address a variety of issues, including consumer protection, anti-money laundering (AML), and know-your-customer (KYC) regulations, governments have been building regulatory frameworks. The governing laws seek to strike a balance between promoting innovation and protecting the interests of consumers and investors.

Comprehensive regulatory frameworks have been put in place to control cryptocurrency exchanges and service providers in nations like the United States and Japan. In order to protect investors while also stimulating innovation, they seek to achieve a balance. License requirements, AML and KYC procedures, cybersecurity precautions, and consumer disclosure duties may all be part of these legislation. Other nations, like Switzerland, have taken a more permissive approach, fostering a supportive environment for cryptocurrency enterprises while also putting policies in place to discourage illegal activity.

While some nations have accepted Bitcoin, others have outlawed or imposed usage restrictions. Initial coin offerings (ICOs), cryptocurrency exchanges, and mining activities have all been outlawed in China, for instance. India initially forbade banks from working with cryptocurrency-related companies, but the Supreme Court later lifted the prohibition. These prohibitions and limitations are frequently brought about by concerns about consumer safety, financial stability, and money laundering.

The regulatory environment for cryptocurrencies in the US is complex. The Securities and Exchange Commission (SEC), the Commodity Futures Trading Commission (CFTC), and the Internal Revenue Service (IRS) are just a few of the regulatory organizations that have issued guidelines and rules specifically for cryptocurrencies. For taxation reasons, the IRS regards Bitcoin as property. Bitcoin payments, mining operations, and gains or losses from these activities must all be reported by individuals. Regulations set by FinCEN (Financial Crimes Enforcement Network) regarding AML and KYC must be followed by cryptocurrency exchanges and service providers.

A regulatory framework has been adopted by the European Union to fight terrorist financing and money laundering. AML and KYC requirements in the EU compel cryptocurrency exchanges and service providers to do client due diligence, keep track of transactions, and report suspicious activity. The General Data Protection Regulation (GDPR) regulations that the EU imposes ensure that personal data is protected in cryptocurrency transactions.

One of the first nations to accept Bitcoin as legal money was Japan. It has strict AML and KYC regulations and has created a licensing system for cryptocurrency exchanges. The legal structure of the nation attempts to advance consumer protection, monetary stability, and the suppression of illegal activity. In order to ensure compliance, the Financial Services Agency (FSA) actively coordinates with exchanges to manage cryptocurrency legislation.

Switzerland has taken a more permissive stance toward cryptocurrencies. By creating clarity and a supportive regulatory climate for blockchain and cryptocurrency enterprises, it has encouraged businesses to establish operations in the nation. In order to combat the threats of money laundering and the funding of terrorism, Switzerland has implemented policies that support both innovation and technological advancement.

The quick development of cryptocurrency presents difficulties for regulators everywhere. Continuous regulatory issues are brought on by the technology's complexity and rapid change, as well as the necessity to achieve a balance between innovation and investor protection. In order to address new challenges like decentralized financing (DeFi), stablecoins, and the international character of cryptocurrency transactions, regulators continue to modify and improve their strategies.

Given the worldwide reach of cryptocurrencies, governments and regulatory agencies must work together internationally to harmonize legal frameworks, fight money laundering, and solve other cross-border issues. The Financial Action Task Force (FATF) and other organizations are working to create international AML and KYC rules for cryptocurrencies.

Governments will probably update and improve their legal frameworks as the cryptocurrency business develops. This might entail creating more precise tax regulations, setting regulatory requirements, and resolving recent concerns like DeFi and stablecoins. Aiming to achieve a compromise between fostering innovation and preserving investor protection and financial stability, legislative improvements will try to promote both.

The main goals of regulatory efforts in the cryptocurrency industry are to safeguard consumers and investors. Regulatory frameworks will probably give priority to steps to fight fraud, increase transparency, and create investor protections as cryptocurrencies become more widely used. This might entail tighter regulation of exchanges, more transparent disclosure rules, and safeguards against market manipulation.

Tax implications and the regulatory frameworks controlling Bitcoin's use are legal considerations. For people and companies functioning in the cryptocurrency field, it is crucial to comprehend tax duties, reporting requirements, and the legal position of Bitcoin. Legal protection as well as the ongoing growth of a reliable and safe ecosystem are both guaranteed by compliance with tax laws and regulatory regulations. Governments will continue to hone their approach to Bitcoin and cryptocurrencies as the world's legal landscape changes, aiming to strike a balance between innovation, consumer protection, and regulatory compliance. The future of the legal framework pertaining to Bitcoin will be shaped by international cooperation and continuous legislative advancements, with the goal of fostering a secure and long-lasting environment for the cryptocurrency business.

CHAPTER
X
Future of Bitcoin and
Cryptocurrency

Expert predictions for Bitcoin's future

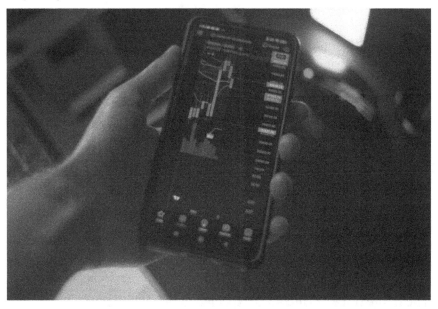

The earliest and most recognized cryptocurrency in the world, Bitcoin, has attracted a lot of interest in recent years. Various predictions about the future of Bitcoin have been made by professionals and analysts as the cryptocurrency ecosystem continues to develop. This section explores professional perspectives and predictions about Bitcoin, looking at elements including price forecasts, market trends, governmental events, and technology advances. People can acquire insight into the probable course of Bitcoin by taking into account these professional viewpoints and can then make well-informed decisions on the cryptocurrency market.

Since its launch in 2009, Bitcoin has experienced price volatility, regulatory difficulties, and advancements in technology. Assessing expert projections for Bitcoin's future requires a foundational understanding of its historical performance.

The price of Bitcoin has increased significantly during numerous market cycles, which are then followed by times of consolidation and corrections. In the past, these cycles have been influenced by the macroeconomic environment, investor sentiment, and adoption.

Numerous analysts believe that Bitcoin's limited supply, decentralized structure, and rising popularity will make it an effective long-term store of value. They contend that factors such as Bitcoin's limited supply, periodic price halvings, and potential acceptance by institutional investors could eventually raise the currency's price.

The future price of Bitcoin is expected to rise significantly, according to several bullish projections made by experts. These forecasts are frequently motivated by elements like growing institutional usage, unpredictability of the global economy, and the possibility for Bitcoin to act as an inflation hedge.

Other experts, on the other hand, have presented more cautious viewpoints, emphasizing the potential dangers and uncertainties related to Bitcoin. They list potential variables that could have a detrimental impact on Bitcoin's price as regulatory difficulties, market manipulation, and the advent of other cryptocurrencies.

Institutional investors, like hedge funds and asset management companies, have entered the Bitcoin market, which has been seen as a significant development. According to experts, growing institutional use may help the cryptocurrency ecosystem gain liquidity, stability, and widespread acceptability.

One significant element that may have an impact on Bitcoin's future is the changing regulatory environment. According to experts, improved monitoring, attractive legal frameworks, and more investor trust may encourage institutional investment in the cryptocurrency sector.

Future Bitcoin developments are influenced by general economic trends. The price and adoption of Bitcoin can be influenced by a variety of variables, including geopolitical events, monetary policy, inflation, and economic crises. These macroeconomic variables are taken into account by experts when projecting the future course of Bitcoin.

The scalability constraints of Bitcoin have generated discussion and concern. However, experts believe that in order to overcome scalability difficulties and increase Bitcoin's transaction throughput, solutions like the Lightning Network, sidechains, and second-layer protocols will soon be implemented.

Another area of technology development is enhancing privacy features in Bitcoin transactions. The anonymity and fungibility of Bitcoin are expected to be improved by the inclusion of privacy-enhancing technology like zero-knowledge proofs and private transactions, according to experts.

By carrying out off-chain transactions, Layer 2 solutions like the Lightning Network seek to increase Bitcoin's transaction speed and lower fees. Additionally, experts predict that the Bitcoin ecosystem will acquire smart contract capabilities, enabling more sophisticated financial applications and decentralized applications (DApps).

Experts predict the emergence of cross-chain solutions and interoperability protocols as the cryptocurrency industry evolves. These developments would make it possible for various blockchain networks to connect seamlessly, increasing the utility of Bitcoin and opening up new use cases.

The regulatory environment that surrounds cryptocurrencies is still uncertain and subject to change. Government regulations may have an effect on how widely Bitcoin is used, how liquid it is, and how people view it. The possible risks connected to regulatory interventions and the requirement for compliance within changing legal framework are acknowledged by experts.

The historical price volatility of Bitcoin is probably going to remain into the future. Due to the possibility of severe price fluctuations and market corrections, experts advise risk management and long-term investing strategies.

Opportunities are provided by technical improvements, but there are risks and uncertainties as well. In order to reduce potential vulnerabilities and risks, experts emphasize the necessity for strong security measures, careful testing of new technologies, and cautious adoption.

Bitcoin's dominance is being threatened by the emergence of alternative cryptocurrencies. The competitive environment and prospective effects of new initiatives and technology on market share and adoption of Bitcoin are taken into account by experts.

The complexity and unpredictability of the cryptocurrency business are reflected in the vast range of expert predictions for the future of Bitcoin. Others place emphasis on the significance of regulatory changes, market trends, and technical breakthroughs. Some analysts predict considerable price rises and sustained institutional use. The past performance of Bitcoin, market cycles, and the dynamic nature of the cryptocurrency ecosystem must all be taken into account when evaluating these professional viewpoints. People can make informed decisions, manage risks, and navigate the shifting landscape of Bitcoin and other cryptocurrencies by learning from expert predictions. In the end, a mix of market forces, technological advancement, legal frameworks, and the continued development of international financial systems will have an impact on the future of Bitcoin.

Bitcoin and the future of finance

The first decentralized cryptocurrency in the world, Bitcoin, has become a disruptive force in the financial sector. Its distinct features and underlying blockchain technology have sparked discussions and speculative thinking about its potential influence on the direction of finance. This section examines how Bitcoin is changing the financial landscape by looking at its possible advantages, disadvantages, and financial implications for many areas of the industry. We can learn more about how Bitcoin is positioned to influence the future of finance by examining these variables.

Due to its scarcity and decentralized structure, Bitcoin has the potential to be a store of value. It is a desirable alternative to conventional fiat currencies and store-of-value assets like gold due to its scarcity and perceived immunity to inflation.

Blockchain technology, which underpins Bitcoin, enables safe, worldwide, and quick transactions. With less reliance on intermediaries, cheaper transaction costs, and quicker cross-border transfers, its potential as a medium of exchange challenges conventional payment systems.

Anyone with internet access can join the network because of Bitcoin's decentralized structure, regardless of geography or financial situation. Through the provision of financial services and possibilities that were previously inaccessible, this has the ability to empower the underbanked and unbanked communities.

The peer-to-peer nature of Bitcoin and its low transaction fees have the potential to completely transform the remittance market. Bitcoin can facilitate quicker and more cheap cross-border transactions by cutting out conventional intermediaries and lowering expenses, which is advantageous to both individuals and businesses.

By providing an alternative financial infrastructure, Bitcoin puts the conventional banking system under pressure. Because it is decentralized, there are no longer any intermediaries necessary, which might save costs and increase efficiency in processes like lending, borrowing, and asset management.

Decentralized applications (DApps) and smart contracts can be made easier by the blockchain technology that powers Bitcoin. Decentralized finance (DeFi), where financial services may be obtained without relying on conventional financial intermediaries, is made possible by this. This encourages transparency and lowers counterparty risk.

Regulators trying to establish precise rules will encounter difficulties due to Bitcoin's decentralized nature. Issues like AML (anti-money laundering), KYC (know-your-customer), taxation, and investor protection are challenges that governments all over the world are trying to solve. Finding a balance between encouraging innovation and reducing risks continues to be a difficult task.

Regulators are progressively creating frameworks to deal with the special features of cryptocurrencies. Some nations have enacted legislation to protect investors and license requirements for cryptocurrency exchanges. The future of Bitcoin and its inclusion into the larger financial system will be determined by how the regulatory environment develops.

The price volatility of Bitcoin continues to be a major obstacle to its widespread acceptance as a reliable unit of account. Price fluctuations may impede Bitcoin's ability to become a widely used form of payment by discouraging businesses and consumers from utilizing it.

The constraints of Bitcoin's scalability have been a subject of debate. As the network expands, questions about capacity and transaction speed are raised. The Lightning Network and layer 2 solutions, among other continuing innovations, are meant to overcome these scalability problems and increase the transaction throughput of Bitcoin.

The safe custody and storage of Bitcoin assets present difficulties. Due to Bitcoin's decentralized nature, users are responsible for protecting their private keys, which, if misplaced or stolen, can result in a permanent loss of assets. Wider usage requires reliable custodial solutions and strong security measures.

Major businesses and financial institutions investing in Bitcoin and providing services related to cryptocurrencies are signs of growing institutional interest in Bitcoin, which indicates a trend toward greater acceptability. Liquidity, stability, and improved public confidence in Bitcoin as an asset class can all be influenced by institutional adoption.

Ongoing technological developments, such as enhanced scalability, privacy, and interoperability, are anticipated to overcome current issues and increase the number of applications for Bitcoin. The underlying blockchain technology may be improved to encourage innovation and open up new opportunities for the financial industry.

The emergence of Bitcoin presents a threat to established financial systems, driving them to innovate and adapt. Because of the popularity of cryptocurrencies like Bitcoin, central banks are looking into the idea of central bank digital currencies (CBDCs). A more inclusive, effective, and transparent financial ecosystem might result from this evolution.

Bitcoin's decentralized structure, cross-border transactions, and innovative technology all contribute to its potential to change the financial landscape in the future. Bitcoin presents prospects for financial inclusion, disintermediation, and efficiency improvements as the financial sector develops. However, issues including pricing volatility, scalability, and regulatory uncertainty still exist. The degree to which Bitcoin is integrated into the traditional financial system will depend on how well regulation and innovation can coexist. Stakeholders may navigate the changing financial landscape and utilize the revolutionary power of cryptocurrencies by embracing the potential advantages of Bitcoin while managing the related risks.

Emerging trends: DeFi, NFTs, central bank digital currencies

Emerging developments in decentralized finance (DeFi), non-fungible tokens (NFTs), and central bank digital currencies (CBDCs) are causing a rapid shift of the financial landscape. These trends have the potential to change a number of facets of finance, including asset ownership, accessibility, and the function of central banks. In-depth analyses of each trend's definitions, traits, advantages, drawbacks, and implications for finance's future are provided in this section. People can obtain insight into the changing financial ecosystem and make wise judgments by knowing these new trends.

Decentralized finance, or DeFi, is a ground-breaking idea that uses smart contracts and blockchain technology to establish a decentralized financial environment. It attempts to do away with intermediaries and offer unrestricted access to financial services. Decentralized exchanges, yield farming, lending and borrowing, and other services are all available on DeFi platforms. Increased accessibility, lower prices, and improved financial control are all advantages of DeFi. To ensure the long-term viability of DeFi, issues including regulatory uncertainty and smart contract weaknesses must be resolved.

NFTs, or non-fungible tokens, have drawn a lot of attention because of their capacity to represent ownership or provide proof of the legitimacy of special digital assets. NFTs provide fractional ownership and new markets for illiquid assets by enabling the tokenization of real-world assets. Through NFTs, creators and artists can directly recover the value of their work without using conventional intermediaries. To ensure the ethical expansion of the NFT industry, however, issues including scalability, environmental concerns, and copyright infringement must be properly taken into account.

Digital forms of fiat money issued by central banks are known as central bank digital currencies, or CBDCs. CBDCs want to increase financial inclusion, offer safe and effective payment methods, and deal with new issues that are coming up in the digital age. There are various CBDC business models, from wholesale CBDCs available only to financial institutions to retail CBDCs open to the general public. CBDCs may provide advantages such quicker and more inclusive payments, more monetary stability, and better regulatory monitoring. However, throughout their implementation, issues including privacy concerns, the need for technological infrastructure, and their impact on commercial banks must be carefully evaluated.

DeFi, NFTs, and CBDCs are three new phenomena that are interconnected components of the changing digital finance ecosystem. These tendencies can work together to produce new financial tools and decentralized asset ownership. To fully utilize the potential of these developments, collaboration amongst stakeholders, including business leaders, legislators, and regulators, is essential. To guarantee consumer safety, financial stability, and compliance with anti-money laundering and know-your-customer standards, clear regulatory frameworks must be established. When it comes to encouraging the responsible adoption and use of these developing technologies, user education and awareness are crucial.

The introduction of DeFi, NFTs, and CBDCs, prompted by technical advancements and shifting customer expectations, signifies a paradigm shift in the financial sector. These developments could revolutionize asset ownership, democratize finance, and alter the function of central banks. To ensure the long-term viability and beneficial influence of these trends, concerns including security, scalability, regulatory frameworks, and environmental sustainability must be addressed. The future of finance may take advantage of the revolutionary power of DeFi, NFTs, and CBDCs to create a more inclusive and effective financial ecosystem by encouraging collaboration, embracing innovation, and finding a balance between risk and reward.

CONCLUSION

Summarize key points of the e-book

The e-book "Bitcoin: Mastering the World of Cryptocurrency - Your Ultimate Handbook on Bitcoin" serves as a thorough reference for anybody looking to comprehend and navigate the cryptocurrency environment and offers insightful information about the world of Bitcoin. The main themes of the e-book will be briefly summarized in this section, with an emphasis on the core ideas, real-world uses, and potential dangers of Bitcoin. Readers can build a strong understanding of Bitcoin and its implications for the future of finance by examining these essential topics.

The e-book opens with a description of Bitcoin as the first decentralized digital currency, emphasizing its innovative technology, secure transactions, and the idea of a distributed ledger known as the blockchain. It explains the mining procedure, which entails resolving challenging mathematical problems to verify transactions and secure the network. With a maximum quantity of 21 million coins, the scarce nature of Bitcoin is further underlined.

The relevance of Bitcoin wallets, which are used to store and manage Bitcoin holdings, is covered in detail in the e-book. It goes over the many kinds of wallets, including as paper, hardware, and software wallets, and highlights each one's unique security characteristics. To guard against potential threats, it is crucial to secure private keys and use best practices, like two-factor authentication and regular backups.

The e-book examines the Bitcoin transaction mechanism and explains how it works with public addresses and private keys. It talks about how Bitcoin transactions are pseudonymous and emphasizes the value of privacy-enhancing techniques like utilizing different addresses for every transaction and using privacy-focused tools like mixers or CoinJoin. The e-book clarifies common misunderstandings about Bitcoin's anonymity and highlights the importance of exercising caution when preserving privacy.

An overview of Bitcoin mining is given in the e-book, along with an explanation of how miners compete to validate transactions and add blocks to the network. It describes how the proof-of-work algorithm, in particular, plays a key role in maintaining the security and integrity of the Bitcoin network. It is also talked about how much energy mining uses and whether there will ever be more energy-efficient alternatives.

The e-book briefly discusses Bitcoin's potential as an investment, stressing both its historical price development and the variables that affect its worth. It covers the ideas of dollar-cost averaging and long-term investing as well as the dangers of short-term trading and market volatility. To make wise investing decisions, it is critical to do in-depth study and comprehend risk management techniques.

The e-book discusses Bitcoin's potential to disrupt established financial systems and change a number of industries as it analyzes its possible effects on the future of finance. It draws attention to how blockchain technology is being used for purposes other than cryptocurrencies, such as smart contracts and decentralized finance (DeFi). The e-book also highlights how crucial regulatory frameworks and widespread acceptance are to Bitcoin's long-term viability and inclusion into the world's financial system.

The e-book "Bitcoin: Mastering the World of Cryptocurrency - Your Ultimate Handbook on Bitcoin" is a thorough guide that covers the essential elements of Bitcoin, from its underlying technology to real-world applications and investing concerns. It gives readers a firm foundation of information they may use to navigate the complicated world of cryptocurrencies and comprehend the possible benefits and risks of using Bitcoin. Readers can learn important insights into the underlying ideas and implications of Bitcoin as a disruptive force in the world of finance by reading this essay's summary of the e-book's main ideas. Understanding Bitcoin's fundamental concepts and real-world applications in depth is crucial as it continues to develop and influence the financial environment.

Final thoughts on mastering Bitcoin and the world of cryptocurrency

The road to mastering Bitcoin and discovering the world of cryptocurrencies is long and full with opportunities and difficulties. This section is a reflection on what was learned and how Bitcoin has changed the financial landscape. It investigates the revolutionary potential of cryptocurrencies, the value of education and awareness, the risks and benefits that could arise, and the prospects for Bitcoin and the larger cryptocurrency ecosystem in the future. We can better understand the significance of Bitcoin and its part in influencing the future of finance by looking into these concluding ideas.

Bitcoin and other cryptocurrencies have the power to completely change the way we engage with financial systems, transact, and store value. Because cryptocurrencies are decentralized, there is no longer a need for intermediaries, giving people more control over their finances. Blockchain technology, which underpins cryptocurrencies, has the potential to improve different businesses' transparency, security, and efficiency. We observe cryptocurrency's transformational power and the potential for mainstream adoption as we become experts in the field.

In order to master Bitcoin and navigate the cryptocurrency world, education and awareness are crucial. People should make an effort to comprehend the basic ideas, the technology, and the dangers related to cryptocurrencies. Knowing more enables us to make wise selections, spot fraudulent endeavors from legitimate ones, and promote the adoption of ethical behaviors. Forging an informed community that can affect good change in the cryptocurrency ecosystem, education programs, academic research, and industry partnerships are essential.

It is important to be aware of the potential risks and rewards associated with the realm of cryptocurrencies as we delve into it. One of the difficulties that calls for caution and risk management techniques is volatility. Other difficulties include regulatory uncertainty and security risks. But it's impossible to ignore the potential benefits, which include financial inclusion, investment opportunities, and technology advancements. The ability to balance risk and reward is essential for navigating this quickly changing environment.

Since its beginnings, Bitcoin and other cryptocurrencies have advanced significantly. Looking ahead, this innovative technology has a promising future. With institutional investors, large organizations, and governments acknowledging the potential of cryptocurrencies, mainstream adoption is still expanding. The scalability and energy efficiency issues that have been a problem for technology are now being solved, allowing cryptocurrencies to handle more transactions and having a smaller environmental impact. A more open and decentralized financial system is made possible by the adoption of cryptocurrencies in daily life, including payment systems and decentralized applications.

As we come to an end with our exploration of Bitcoin and the cryptocurrency industry, it is critical to stress the significance of ethical behavior. People should put security first by using secure wallets, using proper password practices, and being on the lookout for frauds and phishing attempts. To maintain compliance with regulations, it is essential to comprehend the legal and tax implications of cryptocurrency transactions. Additionally, encouraging tolerance, diversity, and moral behavior within the cryptocurrency community helps to create a more just and sustainable ecosystem.

Understanding Bitcoin and the cryptocurrency industry is a lifelong process that calls for continuous learning, flexibility, and an open mind. We recognize the revolutionary power of cryptocurrencies and their potential to change finance as we take a moment to consider the information we have learned. The foundations for responsible participation in this dynamic environment are knowledge and awareness. While there are concerns, it is impossible to overlook the potential benefits and favorable effects. We can support the development and maturity of the cryptocurrency field by embracing ethical behavior and encouraging teamwork. Let us be consistent in our pursuit of knowledge, innovation, and the democratization of finance as Bitcoin and cryptocurrencies continue to develop.

Encouragement for the reader's Bitcoin journey

Starting a Bitcoin journey is a thrilling and transformational effort that has the potential to empower you financially and help you grow as a person. This section seeks to inspire readers on their Bitcoin journey by outlining the opportunities, challenges, and rewards that are still to come. People can travel the road to financial independence and profit from taking part in the Bitcoin world by creating a positive mindset, accepting lifelong learning, and developing resilience.

The journey of Bitcoin is characterized by countless possibilities. It is essential to develop a mindset that values innovation and the possibility of progress. Recognize that Bitcoin is more than just a digital currency; it stands for a fundamental shift in how we interact with financial systems, transact, and hold value. You can explore prospects for professional advancement, technological exploration, and the empowerment that comes from being an early adopter of disruptive technology by accepting the power of potential.

A successful Bitcoin journey requires education and ongoing learning. The cryptocurrency landscape is dynamic and always changing, therefore it's important to be informed in order to make wise decisions and reduce risks. To gain a deeper grasp of Bitcoin's technology, market trends, and regulatory developments, conduct in-depth study, adhere to reliable sources, and make use of instructional tools. By continuing to learn more, you establish yourself as a knowledgeable member of the Bitcoin community who is able to navigate challenges and seize opportunities.

The road to Bitcoin is not without challenges and setbacks. Your resolve may be put to the test by volatility, market swings, and regulatory concerns. However, it is in these trying times when resilience is most important. Accept defeats as opportunities for learning and be ready to adjust your strategies as necessary. Develop risk management techniques that are in line with your financial objectives, make improvements to your investing strategy, and learn from previous mistakes. Keep in mind that setbacks are just temporary, and that perseverance will ultimately make your path stronger.

Bitcoin is more than simply a technology; it is also a community with a common goal. Be in the company of people who share your views and are also exploring Bitcoin. Join online communities, participate in debates, go to conferences, and share your views to gain knowledge from others' experiences. Work together with others to promote change and aid in the expansion and use of Bitcoin. You may grow your network, learn insightful things, and find support for your journey's ups and downs by forming relationships within the Bitcoin community.

The Bitcoin journey is a marathon, not a sprint. It necessitates having a long-term outlook and concentrating on the wider picture. Recognize that it might take years or perhaps decades for Bitcoin's true potential to manifest. You set yourself up for long-term financial empowerment by developing patience and a firm confidence in the revolutionary power of Bitcoin. Recognize that Bitcoin marks a fundamental shift in the way we think about money and decentralization; it is more than just a speculative investment. Keep your eyes on your financial objectives as well as the possible effects that Bitcoin may have on your life and the world around you as you continue on your journey.

Choosing to go on a Bitcoin adventure can lead to financial empowerment, technological exploration, and personal development. You set yourself up for success in the Bitcoin ecosystem by believing in the power of possibility, constantly learning new things, developing resilience, encouraging community and collaboration, and keeping a long-term outlook. Stay persistent in your dedication to financial independence and keep in mind that the experience itself is a worthwhile learning opportunity. Keep an open mind, stay informed, and be prepared to adjust as you navigate the future route. Your experience with Bitcoin has the ability to change and amplify your life. On this thrilling journey toward financial empowerment, embrace the difficulties, rejoice in your successes, and seize the chances that lie ahead.

Thank you for buying and reading/listening to our book. If you found this book useful/helpful please take a few minutes and leave a review on the platform where you purchased our book. Your feedback matters greatly to us.

www.ingramcontent.com/pod-product-compliance
Lightning Source LLC
Chambersburg PA
CBHW071203050326

40689CB00011B/2223